Into All the World

by

Amos R. Wells

First Fruits Press
Wilmore,
Kentucky c2016

Into all the world by Amos R. Wells.

First Fruits Press, ©2016
Previously published by United Society of Christian Endeavor, [1903]

ISBN: 9781621716228 (print), 9781621716235 (digital), 9781621716242 (kindle)

Digital version at http://place.asburyseminary.edu/christianendeavorbooks/46/

For all other uses, contact:

First Fruits Press
B.L. Fisher Library
Asbury Theological Seminary
204 N. Lexington Ave.
Wilmore, KY 40390
http://place.asburyseminary.edu/firstfruits

Cover design by Jon Ramsay

asburyseminary.edu
800.2ASBURY
204 North Lexington Avenue
Wilmore, Kentucky 40390

First Fruits
THE ACADEMIC OPEN PRESS OF ASBURY SEMINARY

First Fruits Press
The Academic Open Press of Asbury Theological Seminary
204 N. Lexington Ave., Wilmore, KY 40390
859-858-2236
first.fruits@asburyseminary.edu
asbury.to/firstfruits

THE FORWARD
MISSION STUDY COURSE

⚜

"Anywhere, *provided it be* FORWARD." — DAVID LIVINGSTONE.

⚜

Edited by **S. EARL TAYLOR** *and* **AMOS R. WELLS**, *as a committee of the interdenominational Young People's Missionary Movement.*

⚜

The following comprehensive series of text-books has been arranged for, each by a writer especially qualified to treat the topic assigned him. For the more important countries two books will be written, one a general survey of missionary history in the land, together with an account of the people and their surroundings; the second a series of biographies of five or six leading missionaries to that country.

INTRODUCTION. Into All the World. A First Book of Foreign Missions. By AMOS R. WELLS. *Published.*

CHINA. General Survey. By REV. ARTHUR H. SMITH, D. D., missionary in Peking and well-known author. *To be published September, 1903.*
Biographical. **Princely Men in the Heavenly Kingdom.** By HARLAN P. BEACH, M. A., F. R. G. S., Educational Secretary of the Student Volunteer Movement and author of a number of most valuable books; a former missionary in China. *To be published September, 1903.*

AFRICA. General Survey. By BISHOP HARTZELL, in charge of the Methodist missions in Africa.
Biographical. **The Price of Africa.** By S. EARL TAYLOR, Chairman of the General Missionary Committee of the Epworth League. *Published.*

INDIA General Survey. By BISHOP THOBURN, the distinguished missionary to India. *Nearly ready.*
Biographical. By WILLIAM CAREY, English Baptist missionary to India, great-grandson of the famous missionary pioneer.

THE ISLANDS. General Survey. By ASSISTANT-SECRETARY HICKS, of the American Board.
Biographical. By S. EARL TAYLOR.

JAPAN. General Survey and Biographical. By Rev. J. H. DeForest, D. D., a well-known missionary to Japan.

PERSIA. General Survey and Biographical. By Robert E. Speer, Presbyterian Foreign Mission Secretary and author of many valuable books.

SOUTH AMERICA. General Survey and Biographical. Announcement later.

KOREA. General Survey and Biographical. By Rev. H. G. Underwood, D. D., missionary pioneer in Korea.

TURKEY. General Survey and Biographical. By Rev. E. E. Strong, D. D., Editorial Secretary of the American Board.

EUROPE. General Survey and Biographical. By Bishop Vincent, at the head of Methodist missions in Europe.

EGYPT. General Survey and Biographical. Announcement later.

BURMA AND SIAM. General Survey and Biographical. By Rev. Edward Judson, D. D., son of the great pioneer missionary to Burma.

HOME MISSIONS will not be in the least neglected. A full and elaborate set of text-books is proposed, covering in successive volumes by specialists the Indians, Negroes, Mormons, Mountaineers, Chinese, and other foreigners among us, and our Island Possessions. Dr. J. M. Buckley will write one of the volumes. Detailed announcement will soon be made.

A JUNIOR COURSE is also proposed, and one or two text-books will soon be announced.

These books are published by mutual arrangement among the denominational publishing houses involved. They are bound uniformly, and are sold for 50 cents, in cloth, and 35 cents, in paper.

Study classes desiring more elaborate text-books are referred to the admirable series published by the interdenominational committee of the Woman's Boards. The volumes already published are:

Via Christi, by Louise Manning Hodgkins. A study of missions before Carey.

Lux Christi, by Caroline Atwater Mason. A study of missions in India.

A text-book on missions in China, by Dr. Arthur H. Smith, — a more difficult volume than the one he is preparing for the Forward Mission Study Course.

KEY TO THE FOLLOWING MAP

Showing where the world's great missionaries labored

1. Carey.
2. Heber.
3. Duff.
4. Martyn.
5. J. C. Lowrie.
6. Butler.
7. Swain.
8. Hall. Nott.
   Newell.
   Rice.
9. Ramabai.
10. Clough.
11. Ziegenbalg.
12. Swartz.
13. Judson.
14. Boardman.
15. Gutzlaff.
16. McGilvary.
17. Perkins.
    Grant.
18. Fiske.
19. Fisk.
    Parsons.
20. Smith.
21. W. M. Thomson.
22. Goodell.
23. Schauffler.
24. Riggs.
25. Hamlin.
26. Falconer.
27. French.
28. Cantine.
    Zwemer.
29. Annie R. Taylor.
30. Rijnhart.
31. Morrison.
    W. Milne.
32. Medhurst.
33. Bridgman.
34. Ashmore.
35. Abeel.
36. G. H. Mackay.
37. J. H. Taylor.
38. Burns.
39. W. Lowrie.
40. Nevius.
41. Mackenzie.
42. Murray.
43. Gilmour.
44. Allen.
45. Xavier.
46. C. M. Williams.
47. Hepburn.
48. Brown.
49. Verbeck.
50. Neesima.
51. Goble.
52. Greene.
53. Bingham.
54. Thurston.
55. Coan.
56. John Williams.
57. Cross.
58. Cargill.
59. Hunt.
60. Calvert.
61. Marsden.
62. Selwyn.
63. Patteson.
64. Geddie.
65. Inglis.
66. Paton.
67. L. H. Gulick.
68. Sturges.
69. Snow.
70. Logan.
71. Macfarlane.
72. Chalmers.
73. Lyman.
74. Munson.
75. Dober.
76. Coke.
77. Austin.
78. Dahne.
79. Hartmann.
80. Boles.
81. Spaulding.
82. Simonton.
83. Chamberlain.
84. Wood.
85. Grubb.
86. J. F. Thomson.
87. Goodfellow.
88. Gardiner.
89. Trumbull.
90. W. Taylor.
91. A. M. Milne.
92. Mongiardino.
93. Penzotti.
94. Jarrett.
95. Peters.
96. Pratt.
97. Erwin.
98. Bryant.
99. J. C. Hill.
100. Rankin.
101. Riley.
102. Stephens.
103. Westrup.
104. Butler.
105. King.
     Robertson.
     J. H. Hill.
106. Prettyman.
     Long.
107. Clark.
108. Cote.
     G. B. Taylor.
109. Vernon.
     Burt.
110. W. H. Gulick.
111. McAll.
112. Chase.
     Willmarth.
113. Sears.
     Oncken.
114. Nast.
     Jacoby.
115. Willerup.
116. Wiberg.
117. Larsson.
118. Petersen.
119. Egede.
120. Stach.
121. Schmidt.
122. Vanderkemp.
123. Moffat.
124. W. Taylor.
125. Richards.
126. Guinness.
127. Wilson.
128. Good.
129. Crowther.
130. Bowen.
131. Lott Carey.
132. Cox.
133. Seys.
134. Payne.
135. Gobat.
136. Krapf.
137. A. Mackay.
138. Hannington.
139. H. P. Parker.
140. Pilkington.
141. Lull.
142. Livingstone.

A
MEMORY
TEST

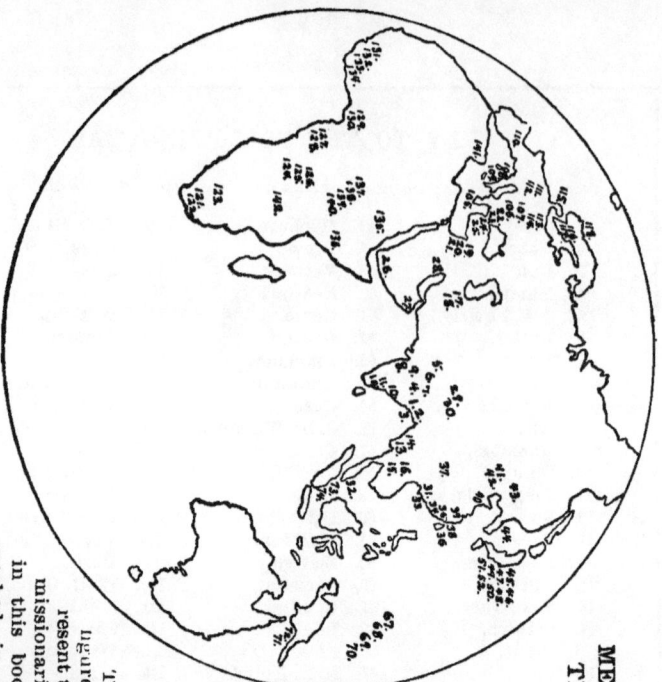

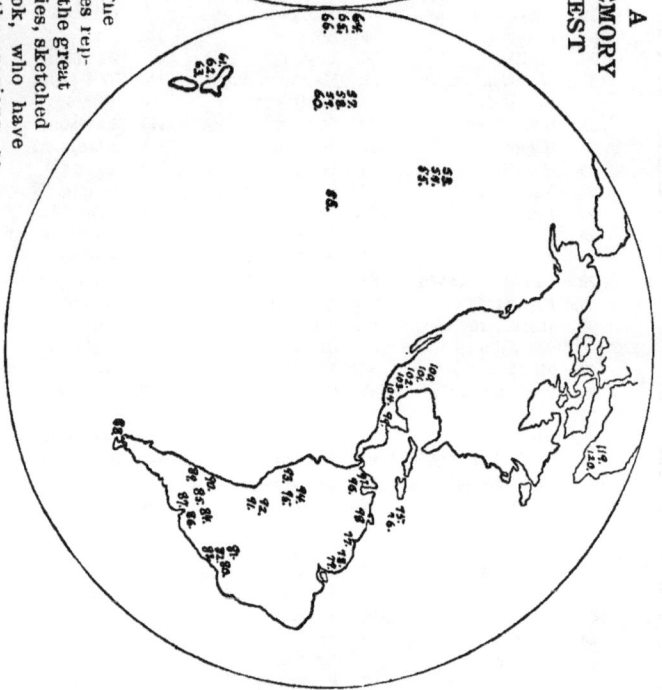

The figures represent the great missionaries, sketched in this book, who have worked in the regions so marked. Try to name them, recalling the chief events of their lives. Consult, when necessary, the key on the preceding page.

Into All the World

By
AMOS R. WELLS

"I am the light of the world."
"The field is the world."
"Go ye therefore, and teach all nations."

BOSTON AND CHICAGO
UNITED SOCIETY OF CHRISTIAN ENDEAVOR

Preface

ENORMOUS difficulties are involved in the preparation of such a book as this, where the field to be covered is the world in space and more than one century in time.

The best authorities have been used, and there has been an earnest endeavor to be accurate in all points, and to observe right proportions. The author has labored under a profound sense of the importance of his task.

In spite of conscientious care, however, it is very likely that specialists in each of the many fields surveyed will discover errors or infelicities. The author earnestly invites all such persons, for the sake of the missionary cause, to write him regarding these points, that the book may become more nearly what it should be.

Let it be kept in mind, however, just what kind of book is aimed at. This is a biographical history of modern missions. It might almost be called an anecdotal history. It is based upon the assumption, true in the writer's case and he believes in most others, that an interest in missionaries is the basis of an interest in missions. An attempt is here made to convey an impression of the great number of beautiful and heroic souls that have wrought to bring the world to its Redeemer. I have tried to show the variety as well as indicate the number of these splendid characters. Under severe limitations of space, I have sought to select, for each brief sketch, not necessarily what Doctor Dryasdust would consider most important, but the deeds and sayings by which the *man* is known and can be remembered. It is somewhat such a scheme that has made Stopford Brooke's " Primer of English Literature," though it treats even more briefly a greater number of persons, so brilliant and effective a text-book.

Attention might be directed to three other purposes of this little book : (1) while relating, as all accounts of missions must relate, the lives of the eminent English and Continental missionaries, yet to emphasize, as no other book has emphasized, the work of our own American denominations ; (2) to show the present distribution of that work ; and (3) to combine missionary history and graphically present it in a series of cumulative chronological diagrams and simple maps that is, so far as I know, unique. I have supplemented these, in the section devoted to class-work, with plans for many more, with lists of the most accessible books of reference, with many suggestions for further study, and especially with sets of test questions on each chapter. These will be of value to the general reader as well as the student in a class.

Amos R. Wells.

Tremont Temple, Boston, Mass.

Contents

Into All the World

I.

THE MISSIONARY CENTURY

There are two ways of looking at foreign missions.

One may say, "It is nineteen hundred years since He whom we call Lord and Master bade His followers go into all the world, and make disciples of all men. It is nineteen centuries since that loving, eager command was given, and see how poorly it has been obeyed!

"In China, among the three hundred and fifty million blind disciples of Confucius, all their wisdom and hope laid level with the grave — in China, out of all those millions, only two hundred thousand have been won to any form of alliance with our Christ who is the Life, and only half of these have joined His living church.

"Of the fanatic, fate-bound followers of Mohammed, two hundred million in number, but the merest handful, a paltry thousand or so, have been led to Mohammed's Lord.

"Throughout the Dark Continent, with its one hundred and sixty million benighted souls, to whom the world is an ambuscade of demons, a light has been set up here and there, but not a million have come to the Light of the World, and whole countries full have as yet caught no least ray of His splendor.

"India's three hundred million, one-fifth of the population of the world for which Christ died, still bow down to wood and stone, and only one in three hundred has drawn near to the God of spirit and truth.

"Nineteen centuries after our Saviour bade us bring the world to the foot of the Cross, and only a million and a half brought thither out of a billion souls! Alas, for our faithless church! Alas, for the doomed world!"

That is one way of looking at missions. It is a common way, but it is not the right way.

We must grant that the church of Christ has been shamefully slow in awaking to its missionary duty. We must acknowledge that even yet it is only half awake.

But that is an element of hopefulness in the situation. Only half a century has Christendom been at all in earnest in this matter. Only during the latter decades of this missionary century has the enterprise begun to receive the attention and the sacrifice it may rightly claim. And if so much has been accomplished in so little time, and with forces so inadequate, we may be sure that as soon as the church determines to do its full duty, the task our Master set us will be found easily possible of fulfilment.

The results already achieved are by no means insignificant.

There are 537 foreign missionary societies, with auxiliaries such as woman's boards.

There are sixteen thousand foreign missionaries, with seventy-five thousand native assistants.

More than five thousand stations are occupied, and twenty-two thousand outstations.

More than twenty-three thousand day schools are conducted by missionaries, with more than a million pupils ; and a thousand higher institutions of learning, with fifty-four thousand pupils.

There are eight hundred medical missionaries, with a thousand hospitals or dispensaries, and they treat every year two and a half million patients.

The one and a half million converts that have been gathered into churches, and the two and a half million adherents that attend churches and have virtually cast in their lot with the Christians, count everywhere for much more than their mere numbers would imply. Just as the Christian nations are the rulers of the world, so these Christians in heathen nations are the men and women of influence, recognized as persons of power, loved, honored, and trusted.

Even when we face the question of money, though it must be admitted that the eighteen million dollars given annually for foreign missions by the Protestants of Christendom looks small beside the billion dollars spent yearly by the United States alone for intoxicating liquor, and the more than six hundred million dollars that we pay for tobacco every year, yet when foreign missions began, or even fifty years ago, eighteen million dollars for missions would have seemed like a section from a fairy tale.

And all missionary figures are rapidly growing.

When Carey went out to India and Judson followed, practically all the world was closed against foreign missions ; now, practically all the world is open to them, and open more and more longingly.

The Bible has been translated into more than four hundred languages and dialects, covering the vast majority of the people of the globe. In 1800 the Bible existed in only sixty-six languages and dialects, covering only one-fifth of the earth's population.

The World's Christian Student Federation has a total membership of eighty thousand students and professors, and thousands of these have been led by the Student Volunteer Movement to consecrate their lives to foreign missions. Two thousand Student Volunteers have already gone to the foreign mission fields.

There are in the world one hundred and forty million Protestant Christians. In the United States alone the church-members possess, it is estimated, twenty billion dollars. If all Christians should lay aside for the Lord's work a tenth of their incomes each year, and use only a fifth of that tenth for the cause of foreign missions, enough missionaries might be sent out to evangelize the world in a single generation. The church will do this some day.

The following pages attempt to pass in review a century of missions. It is the record of the best and bravest the human race has yet achieved. The story will carry us into every land, and it will introduce us to scores of heroes.

The facts are multitudinous and alluring, and choice among them is most difficult. Biography is the clue that will lead us through the labyrinth, and I have made the history cluster around a succession of great lives.

In relating these, I have tried to seize upon the picturesque details, the most rememberable facts, the famous sayings, the characteristic incidents, the classic anecdotes. So far as the narrow limits of space will permit, I have tried to make the reader feel, with each successive name, that he is brought in contact with a splendid man or woman about whom he will wish to learn more.

For this is but a first book of missions. It aims to tell only what *must* be known about foreign missions and their heroes, if one is to be even fairly well informed. The book will have missed its mark very largely if it does not prove for the reader a mere introduction to fresh reading, pointing out numberless paths of study and enjoyment. To that end, at the close of the book are given, for the use of classes and individuals, a great many suggestions for additional study along the line of each chapter, together with a list of easily accessible books.

No reading is so profitable as biography, and no biography is so profitable as missionary biography. No other single line of reading will approach it in the variety and value of the information to which it leads — history, biography, sociology, the characters of nations, and the changing face of the world; and nowhere outside the pages of Holy Writ will one meet with nobler souls.

It is to that feast I invite you in the chapters that follow; and may the invitation lead to the reading of many missionary books, and the leading of many missionary lives.

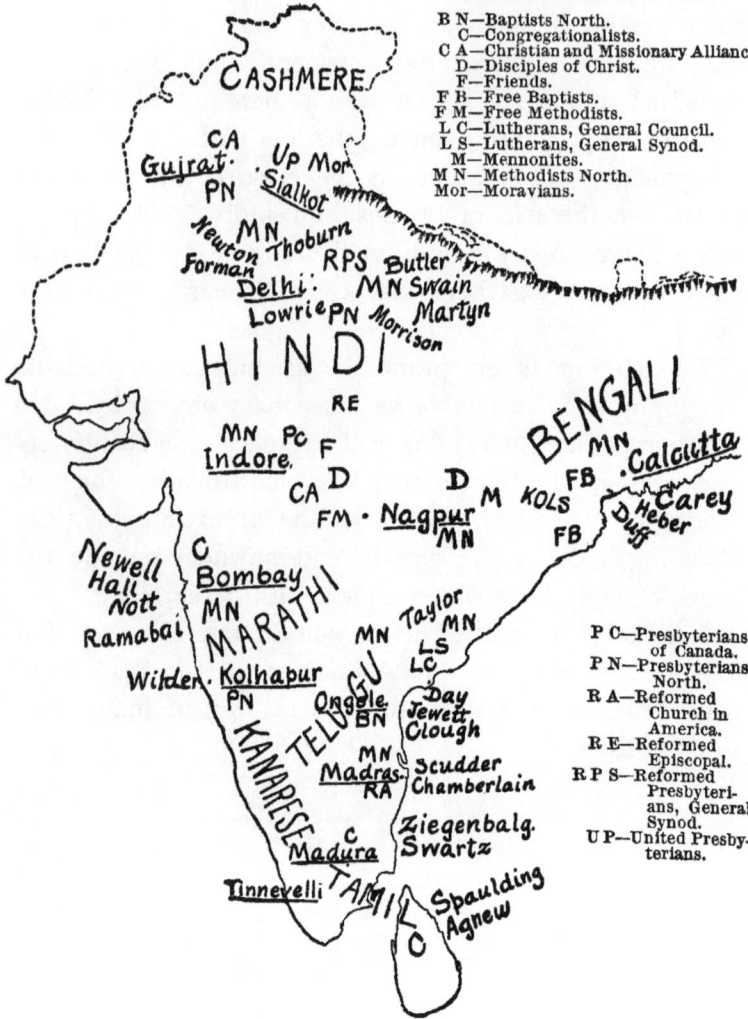

American Missions in India

B N—Baptists North.
   C—Congregationalists.
C A—Christian and Missionary Alliance
   D—Disciples of Christ.
   F—Friends.
F B—Free Baptists.
F M—Free Methodists.
L C—Lutherans, General Council.
L S—Lutherans, General Synod.
   M—Mennonites.
M N—Methodists North.
Mor—Moravians.

P C—Presbyterians of Canada.
P N—Presbyterians North.
R A—Reformed Church in America.
R E—Reformed Episcopal.
R P S—Reformed Presbyterians, General Synod.
U P—United Presbyterians.

CASHMERE

CA Gujrat UP Mor
PN Sialkot
MN Thoburn
Newton RPS Butler
Forman Delhi MN Swain
Lowrie PN Morrison Martyn

HINDI
RE
MN Pc F
Indore CA D
FM Nagpur MN
D M KOLS FB
BENGALI MN Calcutta
FB Carey
Duff Heber

Newell C Bombay
Hall MN
Nott MARATHI MN Taylor MN
Ramabai LS
Wilder Kolhapur Lc
PN Ongole Day
BN Jewett Clough
MN Madras Scudder
RA Chamberlain
c Ziegenbalg
Madura Swartz
Tinnevelli TAMIL Spaulding
Agnew

II.

INDIA

SIZE. — This great empire, about 1,900 miles in length and breadth, is less than half as large as the United States, but contains more than three times as many people, — 294,266,701. Large portions of it contain 400 to a square mile. Great Britain holds direct sway over four-fifths of the population. The remainder (occupying more than one-third of the territory) are ruled by native princes under England's dominance.

RELIGION. — Two-thirds of the people are Hindus in religion. About 60,000,000 are Mohammedans, for India is by far the greatest Mohammedan country in the world. The rest are aboriginal tribes with various religions, Sikhs and Buddhists, with more than one million Christians, more than half of these, however, being Catholics.

LANGUAGES. — The various migrations and invasions that have overrun India have left their traces in a strangely complex population. Including Burma and Siam, the Indian Empire uses three hundred distinct languages and dialects. The most important language-groups, judging by the number of speakers, are the Bengali (around Calcutta), the Marathi (around Bombay), and the Hindi (in the centre and north). Further removed from the primitive Sanskrit are the great languages of the south, the Tamil and Telugu (on the east)

and the Kanarese (on the west).   All of these are culti-
vated languages, possessing their own literatures and
alphabets.

THE CASTE SYSTEM of India constitutes an appalling
hindrance to the gospel.   It originated probably in the
conquest of aboriginal races by more powerful invaders
from the north, and had a fourfold division, — Brahmans
or priests being the highest, then soldiers, merchants,
laborers, and, lowest of all, those without any caste at
all, the outcastes, or Pariahs.   The outcastes may not
live in the villages, nor draw water from the village wells,
nor even touch the lordly beings above them.   This simple caste system, however, has become enormously intri-
cate.   Every trade has its caste, more or less honorable.

THE EAST INDIA COMPANY was incorporated by Queen
Elizabeth early in the seventeenth century, when English
merchants went to India.   The power of this trading
association grew, until Clive won the great battle of
Plassey, near Calcutta, in 1757, and the fall of the ruling
race, the Marathas, on the other side of India, in 1761 ;
the English were then supreme.   The one other great
event in India's history was the terrible mutiny of the
native troops in 1857, which resulted in the passing away
of the East India Company, and the direct rule of the
English sovereign through a governor general.

   This English rule has been just, though stern; it has
greatly developed the resources of the empire, and immense
sums are spent for the relief of the people in times of
famine.   In the famine of 1876–8, for instance, the
government spent $55,000,000 in relief works, notwith-
standing which 5,250,000 persons died.   Since 1804,
when missionary work was officially permitted, Chris-

tianity has had a fair opportunity to move upon the hearts of the people.

BARTHOLOMEW ZIEGENBALG was the brilliant pioneer of Protestant missions in India. When a young man, in 1705, he was sent out with Henry Plütschau by King Frederick IV., of Denmark, to the Danish possession of Tranquebar, in southeast India. The Danish East India Company sent secret instructions to drive him away. He was ridiculed and persecuted, the governor at one time struck him in a rage, he was imprisoned for four months, suffering in the fierce heat, he was often in straits for money, his converts were beaten, banished, killed. He had to learn Tamil by sitting down with the children in a native school, imitating them as they made letters in the sand. The Brahman who afterwards taught him was imprisoned in irons. Slaves alone were permitted to listen to him. His first Bible translation was scratched on palm leaves. Notwithstanding it all, by 1711 he had translated the New Testament into Tamil, — the first translation of Scripture into a language of India; and when he died, only thirty-six years old, in 1719, he left behind him 350 converts, a large mission church, and a native Christian library of thirty-three works.

SWARTZ

CHRISTIAN FREDERICK SWARTZ was dedicated to God by his mother on her death-bed, and at the age of eight he often withdrew from his companions for solitary prayer. When a young man of twenty-two he resigned his patrimony and embarked for India in 1749. Ziegenbalg's mantle soon fell upon the zealous young missionary. For nearly half a century he lived in southern India, instructing the heathen by wonderful conversations, making his home a beautiful orphan asylum, and winning by his saintliness so great esteem from the natives that the Rajah of Tanjore on his death-bed urged him to accept the regency of his country during the minority of his son, and that son, when Swartz died in 1798, erected in his memory a noble monument by Flaxman. After the death of this great man Danish missions in South India sadly dwindled; the permanent beginning of modern missions was in the north.

WILLIAM CAREY, the father of modern missions, was the son of a weaver, and was himself for twelve years a shoemaker. A fellow-apprentice led him to Christ, and he became a Baptist preacher. Preaching was his business, he said, but he cobbled shoes "to pay expenses." His eager mind reached out after knowledge, and, poor as he was, he learned Latin, Greek, Hebrew, Dutch, and French. Early fired with missionary fervor, he kept by his cobbler's bench a large, home-made map of the world, which he covered with notes regarding the religion, population, and condition of the different countries.

CAREY

At a ministers' meeting at Nottingham he preached his famous sermon from Isa. 54: 2, 3, "Enlarge the place of thy tent," etc., the thesis being, "Expect great things from God; attempt great things for God." As a result of this impressive address the pioneer English missionary association (the Baptist Missionary Society) was formed at Kettering, October 2, 1793, and Carey was at once sent to India as its first missionary.

The East India Company compelled him to put back, and he was obliged to set sail in a Danish ship, from Copenhagen. It was Carey's belief that a missionary should be self-supporting, so that he gave up his salary, and he and his family were seriously in want. However, he obtained at last the superintendence of an indigo factory near Calcutta, and for five years worked there, preaching to his thousand laborers, itinerating among two hundred villages, and translating the New Testament into Bengali.

His knowledge of the native languages obtained for him the appointment to the professorship of Sanskrit, Bengali, and Marathi at Fort William College in Calcutta, where he worked for thirty years. His salary was $7,500 a year, but he and his family lived on $200, and gave the rest to his missionary enterprises.

His literary labors were enormous and invaluable. He translated the Bible, in whole or part, into twenty-four languages and dialects of India. This "consecrated cobbler," as Sydney Smith called him in ridicule, gave the Scriptures to three hundred million human beings.

For years he labored for the abolition of the inhuman "suttee," the burning of widows on the funeral pyre of their dead husbands. At last, in 1829, the government sent him, for translation, the proclamation affixing to it the penalty of homicide. Dr. Carey was about to preach, for it was Sunday, but he threw off his black coat, sent another man into the pulpit, and made the translation by sunset. "The delay of an hour," said he, "may mean the sacrifice of many a widow." At the age of seventy-three, on June 9, 1834, he passed away.

THE HAYSTACK MONUMENT at Williamstown, Mass., commemorates the beginning of American foreign mis-

Parallel Events.	Two Centuries of Missions in India.
Boston News Letter. 1704—	—1705. Ziegenbalg. Plutschau.
Peace of Utrecht. 1713—	
George I. 1714—	
Aix-la-Chapelle treaty. 1748—	—1749. Swartz.
	—1757. *Battle of Plassey*.
Wolfe at Quebec. 1759—	—1761. *Fall of Marathas*.
Cook's first voyage. 1768—	
American independence. 1776—	
First Sunday school. 1780—	
French Revolution. 1789—	
Whitney's cotton gin. 1793—	—1793. Carey.
	—1800. Carey's first convert.
Louisiana Purchase. 1803—	—1806. Martyn.
Fulton's steamboat. 1807—	—1808. Haystack meeting.
	—1810. American Board.
	—1812. Judson. Hall. Nott. Newell. Rice.
Waterloo. 1815—	—1823. Heber.
	—1829. Duff. *Law against suttee*.
First locomotive. 1830—	—1833. Lowrie. Reed.
	—1835. Newton.
	—1836. Day.
Victoria crowned. 1837—	—1839. Gossner band.
Whitman's ride. 1842—	
Telegraph. 1846—	—1846. Wilder.
Gold in California. 1848—	—1848. Jewett.
Y. M. C. A. founded. 1853—	—1854. Prayer-meeting Hill.
	—1856. Butler.
	—1857. *Indian Mutiny*.
Atlantic cable. 1858—	—1859. Week of Prayer. Thoburn.
Civil War in U. S. 1861—	—1865. Clough.
Alaska purchased. 1867—	
Suez canal. 1868—	—1870. Swain.
	—1872. Taylor.
	—1883. Ramabai.

sions. In 1808 six students of Williams College formed the first missionary organization in America, writing and signing the original agreement in cipher. They met by night for prayer under a haystack near the college grounds, and there consecrated themselves to the cause of missions. Samuel J. Mills, their leader, had been set apart to the missionary service as a child by his godly mother. Later this centre of missionary enthusiasm was transferred to Andover Theological Seminary, and at Bradford, Mass., on June 27, 1810, a paper was presented to the General Association of Massachusetts, signed by Adoniram Judson,

Samuel Nott, Samuel J. Mills, and Samuel Newell, urging to be sent as missionaries to the heathen. This led at once to the organization of the First American missionary society — the American Board of Commissioners for Foreign Missions.

THE FIRST MISSIONARIES sent out from America were ordained at Salem, Mass., on February 6, 1812. They were Adoniram Judson, Gordon Hall, Samuel Nott, Samuel Newell, and Luther Rice. You may still see the wooden bench on which they sat during the ceremony. On the way to India Judson became a Paptist, and Rice soon joined him, thus starting the great work in a new denomination.

Driven from Calcutta by the hostile East India Company, Mr. and Mrs. Newell found that they must return home or go to Mauritius, whose governor was more friendly to missions. On the way their baby died, and scarcely had they reached Mauritius before Mrs. Newell also passed away of quick consumption — the first American martyr in the cause of foreign missions. Harriet Newell died at the early age of nineteen, and her serene, undaunted faith was a mighty stimulus to the home churches.

After a stay in Ceylon that led later to the establishment of the mission there, Newell joined Hall and Nott, who had managed against governmental opposition to gain a foothold in Bombay. Thus was founded in 1813 the Marathi mission, which with great difficulty maintained its position during our war with England. Five of the ten men sent to that field soon died — Newell and Nott being the first to pass away, the victims of the dread cholera. Now the mission is widely extended through the region around Bombay. Under such leaders as the

Humes and Abbotts it has done a magnificent work, especially in the terrible visitations of plague and famine.

The mission in northern Ceylon was next opened, in 1816, and under such splendid workers as the Spauldings and Miss Eliza Agnew, the veteran and beloved teacher, it has developed especial strength along educational lines. A typical scene was that one night when more than thirty schoolboys were found praying and weeping in a small garden, crying out, "What shall I do to be saved?"

The language spoken in Ceylon is Tamil, and in 1834 the work spread to the Tamils of the mainland, the Madura mission being founded. Here the Chandlers and other noble missionaries have done a great work. It was a happy occasion when on the jubilee of the mission 1,500 Christians with banners and music marched through the streets of Madura, and one thousand adults sat together at the Lord's Supper.

HENRY MARTYN, in his brief life, produced a profound effect for missions. He was an accomplished scholar, "senior wrangler" at Cambridge, fellow of his college, winner of prizes in Latin and mathematics. Converted by the university preacher, Martyn was turned to missions by his praise of Carey and by reading the life of Brainerd.

He was ordained in the Church of England, and became one of the East India

MARTYN

Company's chaplains, reaching Calcutta in May, 1806. He labored, first at Dinapore then at Cawnpore, two places northwest of Calcutta, on the Ganges. Fainting spells and fevers testified to the weakness of his body, and the fierce heat wore him out.

His brave spirit forced him on, however, to labors manifold, — outdoor preaching to the soldiers under a torrid
sky, testifying before the heathen " amidst groans, hissings,
curses, blasphemies, and threatenings," the building of a
church at Cawnpore, and especially translations of the
New Testament into Hindustani and Hindi. He learned
Persian, and translated the New Testament into that
language.

Increasing sickness compelled a sea voyage, and in
1811 we find him at Shiraz in southern Persia, translating
the New Testament into Arabic, holding public and private
discussions with the Mohammedans, and presenting to
the Shah himself a spendidly bound copy of his Persian
New Testament. Again sickness compelled a removal,
and he set out homeward on horseback for Constantinople,
1,300 miles distant. Complete exhaustion overtook him
on the way, and he was obliged to stop at Tokat, in the
centre of Turkey in Asia, where the plague was raging.
There he died, October 16, 1812, at the early age of thirty-
two, and there he lies buried in the Armenian cemetery,
his monument bearing inscriptions in English, Armenian, Turkish, and Persian.

REGINALD HEBER was the greatest of
missionary poets. He was born in England in 1783, and was a most remarkable
boy, reading the Bible readily at the age
of five, begging for a Latin grammar as a
treat at the age of six, and translating

HEBER

Phœdrus into English verse at the age of seven ! He
was generous, and his parents, when they sent him to
school, had to sew his half-year's pocket money into
his clothes, knowing by experience that otherwise he

would give it all away before he reached the school. He was a saintly lad, and would hastily close a book if any expression met his eye that he thought unbecoming.

Heber became a beloved minister of the Church of England, renowned for such poems as "Thou art gone to the grave, but we will not deplore thee," "Brightest and best of the sons of the morning," "By cool Siloam's shady rill," "The Son of God goes forth to war," and especially the immortal missionary hymn, "From Greenland's icy mountains," which he composed in 1819 on the occasion of a special collection for missions taken throughout England.

When called to be Bishop of Calcutta, he shrank from the responsibility, and twice refused it; but his sense of duty prevailed, and in 1823 he set sail for "India's coral strand." His labors were incessant, and sometimes on descending from the pulpit he would be almost unable to speak from exhaustion. Finally he entered upon an extensive visitation of the missions throughout India, and when he had reached the more torrid portions of South India, he suddenly passed away. It was in 1826, after a missionary service of less than three years.

ALEXANDER DUFF, the son of a small farmer, was a pupil of the famous Thomas Chalmers, and grew to be a preacher of ability. When the Church of Scotland decided to engage in foreign missions, he volunteered for the work, and was promptly appointed as its first missionary. The "bad luck" on the ocean that attended him in all his later voyages began when he set sail for India in October, 1829. While the passengers were at a ball on the island of Madeira, their ship was blown out to sea, and could not return for three weeks — a weary time, which had to be spent by all the company — except, of course, Mr. Duff and his wife — in their ball dresses! They were wrecked at the Cape of Good Hope, and again on the coast of Ceylon, and nearly again at the mouths of the Ganges. Thus, after a journey of eight months, in which they lost everything, the missionaries reached Calcutta.

The great fruit of Duff's thirty-five years in India was the founding of educational missions — a principle which he defended

DUFF

powerfully all his life. The mission school he opened became the model for all others. It began with five native students under a banyan-tree. It grew to a splendid institution with a thousand students.

In the education of Hindu women Dr. Duff also made remarkable advances, with his school for high-caste girls opened in the house of a Brahman. All this is more wonderful when we remember that, when the Free Church of Scotland seceded from the Established Church, Dr. Duff went with the former, and built a second great institution from the start — a duplicate of the first.

His schools were true evangelists, and it was a momentous day for India when a company of his high-caste converts met together and solemnly did that terrible deed — ate a beefsteak!

Dr. Duff was the greatest orator the mission cause has produced, and his tours of Scotland and the United States aroused a tremendous interest in missions. In the course of one of these visits home, he wrote in four months a profound work on India, containing about 300,000 words. His labors were enormous, his body weak, and he was compelled in 1863 to return home. His closing years, till his death in 1878, were spent in the work of directing the missions of his church and in teaching missionary theories and practices in the theological seminaries.

JOHN C. LOWRIE and WILLIAM REED, with their wives, were the first missionaries to volunteer in the Presbyterian Church of America. They sailed for India on May 30, 1833. The shouts of the Princeton students aroused Dr. Irenæus Prime, as he lay sick. "Lowrie is off for India," was the explanation given him. Mrs. Lowrie died soon after arriving, Mr. Reed fell ill and died on the return voyage with his wife, so that Mr. Lowrie was left alone to press into the almost unoccupied field of north-western India — a tedious journey from Calcutta that sometimes in those days required more than five months! Lodiana was the first station, and has become the centre of a mission reaching out in all beneficent ways through the Punjab to the west, while to the east Furrukabad has become the centre of another great mission.

JOHN NEWTON, who arrived in 1835, spent 56 years in India, sent there by his mother's prayers, and produced a mighty impression by his powerful personality. One Englishman, thirty years after hearing him read a few verses from the first chapter of Acts, spoke of the wonderful effect that reading had upon him. He was of a most brotherly spirit, and invited the Church of England mission to the Punjab in 1850. He gave his six children to the work, and one of them, JOHN NEWTON, JR., became a famous medical missionary, of whom an associate said, "No love in this dark world has ever seemed to me so much like the Saviour's as that of Dr. Newton for his lepers." C. W. FORMAN was another great Presbyterian missionary of this region. So was JOHN H. MORRISON so fearless in preaching that he was called " The Lion of the Punjab," who, after the terrible mutiny in which four Presbyterian missionaries with their wives and two little children were shot at Cawnpore, led the Lodiana mission to issue a call to Christendom for the first Week of Prayer, which was observed in January, 1859.

ROYAL GOULD WILDER, sailing for India in 1846 under the American Board, founded in 1852 the work at Kolhapur, south of Bombay. The Brahmans petitioned for his banishment, but he stuck at his post, though it was five years before he gained a convert. For twelve years Mr. Wilder sustained an independent mission at Kolhapur, becoming especially prominent in the movement for Indian education. The Presbyterian Church took charge of the mission in 1870, and Mr. Wilder, after completing thirty-two years of mission work, spent the last ten years of his life in founding and editing that periodical so pre-eminently useful, *The Missionary Review of the World.*

SAMUEL S. DAY became, in 1836, the founder of American Baptist missions among the Telugus of Southern India. He labored till 1845 at Nellore, and then had to return home, a sick man. He found the church thinking of giving up the mission, and with an earnest protest he went back to India. **DR. LYMAN JEWETT** joined him in 1848. Still the success of the mission was so slight that again and again it was proposed to transfer it to Burma. It was called " The Lone Star Mission," referring to its solitariness on the map, and Dr. S. F. Smith, the author of " America," did much to save it by writing his famous poem, " The Lone Star." In 1854 Dr. Jewett, with four helpers, held that famous little meeting on " Prayer-meeting Hill " overlooking Ongole, claiming the place for

Christ, and even daring to pick out the site for the future mission house — a prophecy amply fulfilled.

JOHN E. CLOUGH, when this discouraging mission was thirty years old, appeared before the Board, who at first were not inclined to send him out. "What will you do," he was asked, "if we decide not to send you?" "Then I must find some other way to go," he firmly replied. He was sent to Ongole in 1865, and found only twenty-five converts in the whole Telugu country.

CLOUGH

Then came a great famine, in the course of which, being a civil engineer, he employed many thousands of the people upon a government canal, preaching Christ to them all the while. The people began to beg for baptism, but he refused it for months until the famine was over. They persisted in coming, however, and on July 3, 1878, after careful examination, 2,222 Telugu Christians were baptized in a single day. Nine thousand were received before the end of the year, and the largest Baptist church in Christendom was formed in that heathen land. The Pentecost continued. On December 28, 1890, there were baptized at one time 1,671 persons, and these converts have proved themselves to be most devout and faithful Christians.

WILLIAM BUTLER, born in Ireland, was the founder of the American Methodist missions of India. The earnest question, "Do you pray?" asked him by a lady, an

BUTLER

entire stranger, made him a Christian and a minister. After for more than three years his church had been

seeking a missionary for India, he volunteered, going out in 1856.

He chose the upper valley of the Ganges, from which he was at once driven by the great mutiny in which so many missionaries were massacred. His house was burned, and a gallows was built for him. On the retreat he and eighty-six Englishmen held a pass against three thousand Sepoys. His failing health forced him to return to the United States, after ten years of service, only later to found the mission to Mexico.

CLARA SWAIN was the first woman to go as a physician to the women of the East. She began her work, under the Woman's Society of the Methodist Church, in 1870. When the Nawab of Rampore was asked to grant his premises for the work, he at once checked the plea by presenting the estate as a gift to the mission. These beautiful labors for the physical welfare of India's suffering women have opened thousands of doors to the gospel.

MISS SWAIN

WILLIAM TAYLOR, after splendid evangelistic work in North India, established in 1872 the Methodist churches of South India along his favorite lines of self-support. He began with the Eurasians, or half-castes, whose trades formed a financial basis for the churches.

JAMES MILLS THOBURN became, in 1888, the first Methodist bishop of India. He is the son of a godly mother who, when her husband, having twenty dollars left after paying off the mortgage, set aside half for missions and gave her half for a new cloak, said, " Put this with the other ten ; I will turn my old cloak."

He went to India in 1859 at the age of twenty-three, and his magnificent energy and wisdom have built up a great work there. His sister, Isabella Thoburn, was the first missionary sent out by the Woman's Society. When her brother, on account of poor health, was about to return, she reminded him of his call from God to India. "Wait," she urged successfully, "until you have an equally clear call to go home."

THOBURN

Dr. Thoburn established that leading religious paper, *The Indian Witness*, and founded, in a daring evangelistic expedition, the Methodist work in Burma and the Malaysian mission at Singapore. During the last decade the success of Methodist missions in northwest India has surpassed all records in the history of missions — fifteen or sixteen hundred being baptized every year, and the converts coming faster than the available force of workers can give them proper instruction. On a recent trip (1903) in the Punjab, Bishop Thoburn baptized 1,747, and at Thasara held the greatest baptismal service in the history of Methodism, personally baptizing 837 converts.

THIRTY-FIVE AMERICAN SOCIETIES are at work in India, and there is space here only to indicate a few missions, giving some idea of how the ground is covered. The Free Methodists are laboring in north-central India; the Mennonites in the Central Provinces; the Reformed Presbyterian General Synod near Delhi; the Reformed Episcopalians at Lalitpur in the central north; the Moravians in the western Himalayas.

The United Presbyterians founded in 1855 their mission at Sialkot in the extreme northwest, and have tilled with characteristic thoroughness and success the region around, the denomination confining itself to this work and to Egypt.

At Guntur, in the Telugu country, the Lutheran General Synod established in 1842 an important work which has spread throughout that region. The Free Baptists have in India their only mission work, established as early as 1836, and nobly cultivating the field west and southwest of Calcutta.

The Disciples of Christ, beginning in 1882 at Harda, near Indore, have stretched their stations eastward toward Calcutta. The Christian and Missionary Alliance has mission stations in the Punjab and in the north centre toward Bombay. The Presbyterians of Canada work the country around Indore.

The Reformed Church in America labors in the famous Arcot Mission, west of Madras, founded by that glorious missionary family, the Scudders, and noted also for the work of Dr. Jacob Chamberlain and many another magnificent missionary. The Lutherans of the General Council work on the east-central coast. In 1866 the Friends of England sent to India their first foreign missionary, a woman, Rachel Metcalf. The centre of the American Friends' work is now at Hoshangabad, east of Indore.

JOHN GOSSNER, of Germany, became a convert from Catholicism, and threw himself zealously into the work of missions. He believed that men should go forth trusting wholly in the Lord and not relying on human institutions, and was rejoiced when eight young artisans, able to support themselves anywhere, offered themselves to his training for missionary service. He sent them to Australia, and in 1839 he sent out a company to India.

In all, this remarkable man sent out 141 missionaries, his only promise of support being, "I will pray for you."

The greatest success of the Gossner missionaries was granted to their work among the Kols, a degraded, aboriginal race in Chhota-Nagpur, northeastern India. The four missionaries that began the work in 1845 suffered many privations, and were often stoned out of the villages. It was five years before they made their first convert; but after that conversions came in a flood, till ten thousand had been added to the church of Christ — one of the most glorious triumphs of the Cross.

TINNEVELLI, a district in the extreme south, is one of the Pentecostal regions of India. Under the care of the English Episcopalians, the natives have turned to Christ by the thousand. John Thomas was one of the great missionaries in this field. One convert, a Syrian, was stabbed while preaching, but died with the prayer of Stephen, "Lord, lay not this sin to his charge!" In one place an idol, face down, was made the step of a Christian church. One village contained so many desirous of baptism that the village rulers urged the townspeople not to be divided, half heathen, half Christian, and they made it unanimous, even turning their devil temple into a house of God. Sometimes such transformed temples were razed in a night by the enemies of Christianity, and the spot ploughed and sown so that the criminals could plead that no such building ever existed there.

THE LADY DUFFERIN ASSOCIATION is a national institution for giving medical aid to India's women in the only possible way — through female physicians. It had a romantic origin. In 1881, the wife of a native prince in Poona was desperately sick, and the prince sent at last to Lucknow for Miss Beilby, a missionary physician, who cured her. The Maharani, bidding good-by to her new friend, said, " You are going to England, and I want you to tell the good Queen what the women of India suffer when they are sick." She persuaded the missionary to " write the message small " and put it in a locket, which she was to wear around her neck till she could give it to the Queen in person.

The way was opened for Miss Beilby to see Victoria, and that " womanly Queen and queenly woman " was profoundly moved. She took pains to see Lady Dufferin, soon to sail for India with her husband, the new governor-general, and laid the burden on her heart. The result was the formation by Lady Dufferin of a great national association, not distinctively missionary in its character, which confines its efforts to the one aim of training woman doctors and nurses and opening hospitals for the relief of India's women.

PANDITA RAMABAI was taught Sanskrit in her youth, and well trained by her father, a Brahman priest. In the famine of 1874-7 the family went off in the forest to die of hunger — father, mother, and sister. She and her brother wandered to Calcutta, where the brother died. Left alone, the girl's beauty and intellect won friends for her, and she married; but within two years she became that sad being, a Hindu widow — com-

RAMABAI

pelled to shave her head, wear coarse cloth, and be treated like a beast for the rest of her days, and even with the threat of a compulsory life of shame.

A great longing seized her to aid the many millions

of wretched beings in similar plight, especially those hundreds of thousands of little girls who have been "married" to aged husbands, and have become widows for life even before they could speak. She became a Christian in England in 1883, and the noble institutions she conducts are thoroughly Christian, making many converts. At Poona is a school for high-caste widows, while the Mukti mission at Kedgaum shelters two thousand child widows, deserted wives, and famine orphans. The latter establishment began with a single dormitory which the government refused to allow Ramabai to build. "Then," she replied, "I will put up a barn for bullocks and grain." The government afterwards relented, and thus the building was stocked with "grain for the Lord." This is all a work of faith like George Müller's, and in the course of it Ramabai has received many marvellous answers to prayer.

III.

BURMA

BURMA measures about 1,100 miles from north to south, and 700 from east to west. After three wars, Great Britain has annexed to India first Arakan, the western coast region, in 1826; then the rich province of Pegu, around Rangoon, in 1854; and all upper Burma in 1885. The population is nearly seven million, the majority being Burmans; the rest being highland Shans, the various tribes of Karens and other hill tribes, and immigrants from China and India. Ninety-two per cent of the people are Buddhists, and all males must pass some time in a monastery. Burma is the leading Buddhist country of the world.

ADONIRAM JUDSON, born in 1788, the son of a Congregational clergyman, became the pioneer of American foreign

JUDSON

missions. When only three years old, he surprised his father one day by reading to him a chapter in the Bible. When four, he would gather the children of the neighborhood to preach to them, and his favorite hymn was, "Go, preach my gospel, saith the Lord."

When a young man, however, he became infatuated with infidelity, but was turned from it by a singular happening. He was at a country inn, and in the next room was an unknown young man who spent the night in groans, and by the morning had died.   Judson learned to his horror that it was the young man whose arguments had led him into infidelity.

Immediately he entered the theological seminary at Andover, and he had not been there long before he began to think of the mission field — a purpose that spread among his comrades and led to the formation of the American Board.   On February 19, 1812, with his young wife, he set sail from Salem, bound for Calcutta.   On the long voyage around the Cape of Good Hope he became a Baptist — a step which for a time cast him adrift, but led in the end to the formation of the second great American society, the Baptist Missionary Union, and to the spread of the missionary spirit throughout that denomination.

Carey welcomed them to Calcutta, but the East India Company, fearing a religious war with the natives, would not allow them to remain.   After long and disheartening wanderings, beaten about from place to place, even as far as the island of Mauritius near Madagascar, the chance of a ship going thither brought them to Rangoon in Burma, where they landed June 13, 1813.

In after years, when asked about the prospects for the conversion of the heathen, Judson made his famous reply, "They are bright as the promises of God."   In that spirit of faith the great man labored in Burma till his death in 1850.   Eagerly desiring to preach, yet he spent long years in the strategetical work of translating the Bible into Burmese, and preparing a dictionary of the language.

The most dramatic experience of his career was his seizure during the war in which England conquered Burma.   He was thrown into the crowded death prison, where for seventeen months he was confined, laden with fetters whose marks he bore to his dying day, in stifling air, amid horrible filth and vermin, compelled to sleep on his shoulders with his feet drawn high in the air, and tortured with the constant expectation of death. He suffered agonies from heat, hunger, and fever. His precious translation of the Bible, sewed into a pillow, was providentially saved by a Christian native, who had taken the pillow as a memento of the friends he expected never to see again. Judson's heroic wife ministered to him from the outside as best she could, and died soon after the close of those terrible days. Judson was thrice married, each time to a woman of remarkable brilliance and most noble character.

It was six years before Judson won his first Burman convert, Moung Nau, but he lived to see the gospel firmly planted in the English possessions, especially at Moulmein.

GEORGE H. HOUGH and his wife were the first Baptists from America to follow Judson. They were sent out in 1816, the Baptists hav-

—1793. *Carey in India.*

—1806. *Martyn in India.*

—1813. Judson in Burma.

—1816. Hough.

—1818. Colman.
      Wheelock.

—1821. Price.

—1825. Boardman.
—1826. *England annexes
      Arakan.*

—1837. *Victoria crowned.*

—1850. Judson dies.

—1854. *England annexes
      Pegu.*

—1878. Methodists at Rangoon.

—1885. *England annexes
      Upper Burma.*

THE COURSE OF BURMAN MISSIONS.

ing organized their mission board in 1813, as soon as they received Judson's summons to the missionary enterprise. Mr. Hough was a printer, and much was expected from his press, but at the outbreak of the war, disheartened by persecution, he left the country; later, however, he returned. REV. JAMES COLMAN reached Rangoon in 1818, with REV. EDWARD W. WHEELOCK; the first, to die within four years, and the second, even earlier, to commit suicide in the delirium of disease. REV. JONATHAN PRICE, M. D., who came in 1821 to the aid of the lonely missionary, was imprisoned with Judson, and after the war became physician to the Burman king.

GEORGE DANA BOARDMAN was the son of a Maine clergyman. He was a college teacher, with a prospect of the presidency, when he read of the lamented death of James Colman in Burma. "Who will fill his place?" he asked himself; and instantly answered, "I will!"

He reached Burma in 1825, at the time when the war with England was distracting all missionary work. He became the founder of the two great missions at Moulmein and Tavoy. At one time the lonely missionary house was plundered of all its valuables, murderous eyes watching the missionaries through great slits cut in the curtains of their bed.

A wonderful work sprung up among the gentle race of Karens, oppressed and enslaved by the Burmans. Ka Thah-byu, the first convert, became "The Apostle to the Karens." A white man had left among them a book, which they had ignorantly worshipped. Mr. Boardman found it to be the English Prayer Book, which he used as a starting point of his teaching.

With a feeble body, the missionary made arduous journeys through the jungles, often on foot, drenched by the rain, sleeping in the native huts. Everywhere the eager Karens crowded to the gospel. Then came the rebellion of Tavoy, and the seeds of disease were quickened by Boardman's close confinement with three or four hundred persons in a little six-room house with damp walls. Perhaps the most pathetically glorious scene in missionary annals is that of the young missionary — he was only thirty — yielding to the solicitations of the Karens, and being borne on a litter into the jungle to witness the final results of his labors, the baptism of sixty converts. Thus in 1831 Boardman passed away, and, as Judson said, " He fell gloriously in the arms of victory."

BAPTIST MISSIONS in Burma, steadily pushed since the days of Judson and Boardman, now include definite labors for all of the forty-seven tribes and peoples that make up the complex population of the land. The entire country is thoroughly tilled. The result is a church-membership of more than 41,000, of whom 35,000 are Karens, these representing a Christian population of 134,000. There are 700 churches, 500 of which are entirely self-supporting. In 1865 these Burman churches organized themselves as the Burman Baptist Missionary Convention, and they in their turn are sending out Christian missionaries — the final stage in the religious development of a people. The Baptist College at Rangoon has more than 500 students, and the theological seminary at Insein is the largest in all Asia.

No other work for Burma is carried on by American societies except the mission of the Northern Methodists established at Rangoon in 1878.

IV.

SIAM

SIAM possessed 300,000 square miles before its cession of 110,000 square miles to France in 1896. It possesses now only about 200,000 square miles — an area a little less than that of Germany, and 60,000 square miles smaller than Texas. The population is about 5,000,000, equalling that of New York and Chicago. About half of these are Siamese in the south, an indolent, gentle race, without much strength, while the north is occupied by the Shans and Laotians, who are nearer the primitive stock. There is, besides, a great influx of Chinese.

The state religion is Buddhism, and all males must enter the priesthood for a time. Buddhism is found here in strict purity, and the king is its official defender, yet since 1851 the royal favor has been shown most conspicuously and practically to the American missionaries. Before that time the king was a usurper, and had bitterly opposed the missionaries. His nephew, the rightful heir, was compelled to become a Buddhist priest, and in the monastery this prince, Chow Fa Monghut, had obtained for his private tutor an American Board missionary, a Presbyterian, Rev. Jesse Caswell, who won him over not to personal Christianity, but to favor our religion heartily in his realm when he came to the throne in 1851. When the missionary died, the king placed a monument over his grave, and sent to his widow presents amounting to $1,500.

EARLY MISSIONS in Siam were conducted by a number of bodies that for various good reasons afterward abandoned the field to its present, practically sole occupants, the Northern Presbyterians. Gützlaff, together with Tomlin of the London Missionary Society, visited Bangkok in 1828, and sent to America an earnest appeal for missionaries by the same ship that brought the Siamese twins.

In response, Abeel, of the American Board, began his work here in 1831. Rev. William Dean of the Baptists came in 1835. Dr. Ashmore came in 1851. Indeed, all the early Baptist missionaries to China served an apprenticeship in Siam. In 1849 the American Board closed its mission, and in 1869 the Baptists suspended their Siamese work, though they still maintain in Bangkok a mission to the Chinese.

In the English Straits Settlements, at the south end of the Siamese peninsula, the famous missionaries to China, Milne, Medhurst, and Legge, did their work

—1793. *Carey in India.*

—1813. *Judson in Burma.*

—1828. Gutzlaff.

—1831. Abeel.

—1835. Dean.

—1840. Caswell. Buell.

—1847. Mattoon. House.

—1851. *Chow Fa Monghut King.*

—1856. *First treaty.*

—1859. Nai Chune baptized.

—1867. McGilvary to the Laos.

MISSIONS IN SIAM.

while the Flowery Kingdom was still closed. The Methodists have a flourishing mission there, largely self-supporting, with at Singapore an important school for the Chinese that has had more than a thousand pupils in a single year.

THE PRESBYTERIANS established their mission in Siam in 1840, the pioneer being Rev. William Buell. Rev. Stephen Mattoon and Rev. S. R. House, M. D., followed in 1847. Dr. House, in the first eighteen months, prescribed for more than 18,000 patients. Mr. Mattoon so won the confidence of the Siamese that when in 1856 Townsend Harris negotiated the first treaty on behalf of the United States, they insisted upon having the missionary as the first American consul. " Siam," said Consul-General Seward, " has not been disciplined by English and French guns as China has, but the country has been opened by missionaries."

It was not till 1859 that the first Siamese convert, Nai Chune, was baptized. He was often offered lucrative offices, but preferred to support himself as a physician, that he might be more free to preach the gospel.

DANIEL McGILVARY, " The Apostle to the Lao," went to Siam in 1858. In offering himself for the work, he had asked to be sent where others were less inclined to go. In 1867 he was sent to open up the Laos mission. This meant a three-months' perilous journey up the rapids of the Meinam River. His first convert, Nan Inta, was a learned man who was won by the occurrence of an eclipse which the missionary had predicted.

The Laos king opposed McGilvary, even attributing to him a famine that had occurred before he arrived! When his over-lord, the king of Siam, refused to remove the missionary, the king seized two of the converts, hung them up by the ears, and clubbed them to death. Soon afterward, however, the Laos king died, and since then the mission has enjoyed great favor and success.

V.

TIBET

TIBET is the loftiest country in the world, having, it is said, an average elevation above the sea equal to the height of Mt. Blanc. It is four times as large as New England and the Middle States, and has a population of about six million. The people are Mongolians, tributary to China.

The leading religion is Lamaism, a form of Buddhism, the "Grand Lama" being an incarnation of their deity in the form of a living boy, whose palace is at Lhasa, the capital. Tibet is the land of priests; it is said that there is one for every family. It is the land of enormous monasteries and of "prayer wheels."

Thus far Tibet, above all other lands, has successfully resisted the onward march of civilization and of Christianity. The Catholics have made courageous attempts to enter the country, and for a time their missionaries were received with favor, but in the end they were all driven out or slain.

MISS ANNIE R. TAYLOR is the heroine of Tibetan missions. She is an Englishwoman, born in 1855, and was led to the missionary ideal by an address made by Moffat's son. Against her father's opposition, she sold her jewels, and with the proceeds studied medicine at a hospital in London. In 1884 she sailed to China as a missionary of the China Inland Mission. After three years of medical service, she began to long toward Tibet, but it was not till 1892 that the dream was accomplished and the intrepid woman, accompanied by a youth from Lhasa, whom she had healed, set out westward from the Chinese frontier.

She was robbed, many attempts were made to murder her, she lost her way among the mountains, she was often on the verge of starvation; but before the government turned her back she had penetrated within three days' journey of Lhasa, claiming every foot of the road for Jesus Christ. "I am God's little woman," she wrote in her diary, "and He will take care of me."

In 1898 Miss Taylor's journey was repeated by the Scandinavian missionary, Peter Rijnhart, with Dr. Susie C. Rijnhart, his noble wife. They came within 150 miles of Lhasa, burying on their way their infant child, when the husband one day disappeared, having been killed by the Tibetans, and after a thousand terrible experiences Mrs. Rijnhart reached a mission station in West China.

Miss Taylor's Tibetan Band of the China Inland Mission is now laying siege to the Forbidden Land from the Chinese province in the east, the Missionary Alliance on the northeast, and other societies on the frontiers of Assam and India.

Among these are the Moravians in Little Tibet. At great risk they have made several vain attempts to enter the country. They have the New Testament and part of the Old all ready in the language of the people, and they have formed a union to pray for the opening of the country to the gospel.

OTHER ASIATIC LANDS which are practically unoccupied by missionaries are : Siberia, larger than all Europe,
and containing thousands of Russian nonconformists that
will make good Protestant Christians some day; Turkes-
tan, where the Swedes alone have begun to work; Afghan-
istan, where the English carry on hazardous and infrequent
labors through the natives; Baluchistan, with a single
station of the Church Missionary Society; and French
Indo-China, with its great population of 22,400,000, where
only the colporteurs of the British Bible Society are at
work, with an occasional excursion made by the Presbyterian missionaries from Laos on the west.

VI.

PERSIA

PERSIA has an area of 628,000 square miles, ten times that of the New England States. Its population, perhaps nine million, is only one and a half times that of New England. The greater part of the country is a plateau with few rivers and forests, a cold winter and a hot summer. Earthquakes and terrible famines are frequent, and the people are very poor.

The people in the towns and on the farms are mostly descendants of the ancient Persians, while the wandering pastoral tribes are Turks, Kurds, Arabs, and Luurs, or nomad Persians. Women are secluded, and are slaves to men. Taxation is heavy, and the Shah is an irresponsible tyrant. Ninety per cent of the people are Shiite Mohammedans, holding, in opposition to the orthodox Sunnites of Turkey, that the proper successor to Mohammed was Ali, his son-in-law and cousin. The Babists are a secret sect of reformers; the Sufis, among whom were Hafiz, Sadi, and Omar Khayam, are mystics and theosophists; and the Parsees, found, however, chiefly in India, are the followers of Zoroaster and the inheritors of the ancient fire worship.

THE FIRST PROTESTANT MISSION to Persia was that of the Moravians, who began work among the Parsees in 1747, but remained only two years. In 1811 Henry

Martyn came from India, and for nearly a year preached boldly in Shiraz, completing his translation of the New Testament into Persian, and imprinting his lovely character upon many minds.

JUSTIN PERKINS was the pioneer of present-day missions in Persia, sailing under the American Board in 1833. It was decided to found a mission for the Nestorians, and Oroomiah was the chosen spot. The Nestorians are Christians, but of an ignorant and superstitious type, with no proper understanding of the nature and work of Christ. They are the followers of Nestorius, a bishop of Constantinople, who was excommunicated in 431 A. D. They speak Syrian, and their chief bishop is called "Patriarch of the East." Besides the Nestorians in Persia, there are perhaps twice as many across the border in northeastern Turkey.

Dr. Perkins and his co-laborers at first made no attempt to preach, but merely established training-schools for the young. By 1840, however, the Nestorian bishops themselves began to beg them to

—1747. The Moravian attempt.

—1793. *Carey in India.*

—1811. Martyn in Persia.
—1813. *Judson in Burma.*

—1828. *Gutzlaff in Siam.*

—1833. Perkins.
—1835. Grant.

—1843. Fiske.

—1862. Separate from Nestorians.

—1872. Bassett.

MISSIONS IN PERSIA.

preach in their churches, and the first great revival came. The bigotry and corruption of the old church made it necessary at last to establish reformed churches, and the beginning of that movement came in 1862.

ASAHEL GRANT, a Presbyterian physician of Utica, N. Y., was turned toward the mission to the Nestorians when the American Board held an annual meeting in his city. In 1835 he set sail, and reached Oroomiah with Dr. Perkins. He became a mighty physician, especially successful in cases of ophthalmia, so that often those that went to him blind returned seeing. He made many journeys among the bloodthirsty Koords, visiting

GRANT

almost inaccessible mountain regions, and often in peril of his life. His wife and two daughters died, and he himself nearly died with cholera, but he persevered.

He began a magnificent work among the mountain Nestorians, but it was all broken up by the savage attacks of the Turks and Koords, who destroyed their ancient churches, slaughtered them by the hundred, enslaved them by the hundred, and drove the remainder to the plain. It was while ministering to these that Dr. Grant himself died, in 1844, of typhus fever. "I have lost my people in the mountains," cried the Nestorian patriarch, "and now my dearest friend is gone — what shall I do?"

FIDELIA FISKE, who gained much of her missionary enthusiasm from Mary Lyon, reached Oroomiah in 1843, being the first unmarried woman to enter that field. When the missionaries had reached Persia in 1835 there was only one woman in Oroomiah that could read. The

day school for girls that Mrs. Grant had opened, Miss
Fiske transformed into a boarding-school, that the girls
might be removed from their evil home
surroundings. The first Syriac word she
learned was "daughter," and the next
was "give," so that she could say, "Give
me your daughters."

The seminary she founded did a wonderful work. Three hours a day the pupils
FIDELIA FISKE   spent in unwearied study of the Bible.
Almost all that came within Miss Fiske's influence
became Christians. One Koordish chief, a vile and
desperate character, brought his daughter to the
school, and was converted before he left the premises.
All he could say was, "My great sins! My great
Saviour!"

Within the first nineteen years, the seminary enjoyed
twelve revivals. Often the scholars would spend the
entire night praying for their relatives.

Miss Fiske would do itinerant work among the villages
during her vacations. At one of these meetings she was
very tired and longed for a rest for her back, when a
woman seated herself behind her and asked Miss Fiske
to lean upon her. When the missionary hesitated, she
said, "If you love me, lean hard." "That woman," said
Miss Fiske, "did preach me such a good sermon!" But
indeed the missionary always leaned hard upon the
Master whom she loved.

After fifteen years of arduous labors, the missionary's
health gave out, and amid the universal lamentations of
the Nestorian women she was compelled to return
to America, where she died in 1864, aged only forty-eight,
her last words being, "Will you pray?"

THE PERSIAN MISSION was transferred in 1871 to the Presbyterians North, who are the only American workers, and by far the most important of all agencies at work in the country. In 1872 Teheran was occupied by **REV. JAMES BASSETT,** and a mission to the Moslems and Armenians was begun. At one time the Moslems came so eagerly to the mission that the government became alarmed, and ordered the meetings to be given up. At times the majority of boys in the Teheran boys' school are Moslems, and many of them the sons of officials.

Tabriz was occupied next, and in 1892 for a time the government locked up the church and school, putting red sealing-wax over the keyholes. Hamadan, occupied in 1881, possesses the traditional tomb of Mordecai and Esther, and one of the two churches of the mission there is composed of converted Jews and Moslems.

It requires great courage for a Moslem to stand up for Christ. Mirza Ibrahim, one of the Moslem converts, was taken before the governor of Oroomiah in 1892. When cruelly beaten, he only cried with delight, " So was my Saviour beaten." Thrown into a dark dungeon, he was chained to the worst of criminals. As he spoke of Christ to them, they kicked him and choked him so that he died from his injuries. " How did he die ? " asked the crown prince, and his jailer answered, " He died like a Christian."

VII.

SYRIA

PLINY FISK and **LEVI PARSONS** of Massachusetts became the pioneer missionaries to Syria. Both of them, before leaving this country, were instrumental in arousing much missionary interest by their journeys and addresses, the first in the South and the second in the North. They set sail for Smyrna in 1819, and Mr. Parsons went straightway to Jerusalem — then a hazardous journey on account of the unsettled state of the country. After gaining an idea of the conditions there, the missionary sailed for Scio, falling into great danger from Turkish ships of war, and learning on the way of the terrible massacre at Scio in which the Turks butchered 20,000 men, women, and little children, many of them Greek Christians. Still in the pursuit of health, the young missionary — not quite thirty — sailed for Egypt, where he soon died, in 1822.

Mr. Fisk's work was interrupted by Turkish outrages, sometimes a single day witnessing several hundred assassinations in Smyrna. He became a missionary explorer, visiting Egypt, the Holy Land, and Syria, everywhere bearing witness for the truth, and at last closing his brief but noble career in Beirut in 1825, three years after the death of his co-laborer, Parsons.

ELI SMITH, who went to Syria in 1827, was the founder of the great mission press at Beirut, superintending the

50

cutting of the beautiful Arabic type, overseeing the work of printing in all its details. His prime achievement, for he was acquainted with many languages, and spoke Arabic as if it were his mother tongue, was the translation of the Bible into Arabic. The New Testament and about half of the Old Testament was translated, and after his death one of the most satisfactory of missionary versions was completed by Dr. C. V. A. Van Dyck, whose Arabic works number twenty-five.

WILLIAM McCLURE THOMSON led a missionary life whose appropriate monument is his great work, "The Land and the Book," a classic description of the Holy Land. Sailing in the service of the American Board, he reached Beirut in Syria in 1833. The country was ruled by Ibrahim, son of the famous Mohammed Ali, pasha of Egypt, who was finally driven from the country by Turkey. During this war Dr. Thomson was im- THOMSON prisoned as a spy, and his wife, living in a cellar with the cannon balls crashing into the upper part of the building, and suffering also the horrors of an earthquake, received a nervous shock and soon after died.

In the Lebanon region, and chiefly in the northern part, are the Maronites, a peculiar antique sect that pay allegiance to the Roman Catholic church. "The Martyr of Lebanon" was Asaad Shidiak, a Maronite who became a Protestant, was imprisoned by the Catholics, walled in, starved to death, and his body rolled down the mountain side.

In the southern part of Lebanon are the Druses, a fanatical sect somewhat akin to Mohammedans. Difficulties between them and Maronites culminated in the massacres of 1860, in which 15,000 of the Maronites and other Christians were butchered; and Dr. Thomson and the other Protestant missionaries gained a foothold among the Maronites by caring for the fugitives during these troublous times. In 1894, at the age of eighty-seven, Dr. Thomson died in Denver, whose surroundings reminded him of his beloved Syria.

THE SYRIAN MISSION, thus founded, was transferred in 1870 to the Northern Presbyterians. The central stations are four: Beirut, Lebanon, Tripoli, and Sidon. At Beirut is the Syrian Protestant College, one of the most useful institutions in all Asia, with forty teachers and more than six hundred scholars. There, also, is the exceedingly important mission press, which turns out nearly thirty million pages a year.

VIII.

TURKEY

TURKEY, including its African possessions, Tripoli and Bengazi, has an area of 1,111,741 square miles, and is one-third as large as the United States. If we include Egypt and the European countries under Turkish influence, we add half a million square miles, making Turkey about half as large as our own land. European Turkey proper is as large as New England, but Asiatic Turkey is ten times as large.

Occupying this great and varied region are twenty-four million people as varied as the land. The strongest element — about nine million — are Ottomans, Osmanli Turks — the wild Tartars, civilized by Persian and Arabian culture, a brave, polite, industrious, able, but fanatical race. They are Sunnites, or orthodox Moslems, holding that Mohammed's successor should be elected, and not follow in the line of his family. They possess great wealth, three-fourths of the city property in Turkey being said to belong to the church. The few converts made from the Moslems become Christians often at the risk of their lives, and always with the loss of position, friends, and opportunity for advancement; and this, though there is nominal liberty to profess Christianity. The Arabs, the Kurds of Asia, and the Albanians of Europe, are also Moslems. So also are the independent race of Circassians on the Russian border.

The most numerous body of Christians are the Greeks, who are descendants of the ancient Byzantine church, the Eastern or so-called Orthodox division of the Catholic church, which was set off against the Western, Latin, or Roman Catholic church. There are about two million of these, and· about one million and a quarter Armenians, an ancient race whose form of Christianity originated from the teachings of Gregory, so that they are called Gregorians. Their services are very much like those of the Greeks, but the two races are very distinct. The commerce of Turkey is largely in the hands of Greeks, the trade and banking in the hands of Armenians, while these two Christian races possess the brains and enterprise of the nation. It is from these so-called Christian churches that Protestant converts have chiefly been obtained. Their worship is conducted in an obsolete dialect that makes it meaningless to the people, and they possess little spirituality or understanding of the vital truths of Christianity.

—1315. Lull killed.

—1793. *Carey in India.*

—1813. *Judson in Burma.*

—1819. Fisk and Parsons in Syria.
—1822. Goodell sails.

—1827. Smith.
—1828. *Gutzlaff in Siam.*

—1831. Goodell in Constantinople. Schauffler.
—1833. *Perkins in Persia.* Thomson. Riggs.

—1838. Hamlin.

—1846. First American Church at Constantinople.

—1856. The Hatti-Humayoun.
—1858. Bulgarian mission begun.
—1860. Maronite massacres.
—1862. Merriam killed.

—1886. Falconer in Arabia.

—1891. French. Cantine. Zwemer.
—1894. Armenian massacres.

—1901. Miss Stone captured.

MISSIONS IN TURKEY, SYRIA, AND ARABIA.

WILLIAM GOODELL, born in a pious Massachusetts home, was a delicate boy, and permanently injured his spine by walking sixty miles to school at Andover with his trunk strapped on his back. When called to recite, he repeated verbatim the first three pages of the Latin grammar, fine print and all. No wonder he became a great scholar.

GOODELL

In 1822 he set sail as a missionary of the American Board for Beirut, where the war between Greece and Turkey rendered matters so insecure that for two years the missionary seldom went to bed without planning means for escape. From 1831 nearly to his death in 1866, Mr. Goodell labored in Constantinople. The great fire burned his books and other property at the very start. He passed through a plague which claimed from six to ten thousand victims weekly. Fierce persecutions tested his converts. At last, in 1856, the Sultan issued the Hatti-Humayoûn, the edict of religious liberty. During these years Goodell preached in six different languages, and translated the entire Bible into the Armeno-Turkish — a masterly achievement which was the crown of his life.

WILLIAM GOTTLIEB SCHAUFFLER, born in Stuttgart, was led to Christ by a reformed Catholic priest, and was turned to missions by the enthusiastic Wolff, with whom he went to Persia. Desiring something more stable than the incessant journeys of that restless missionary traveller, Schauffler turned to America, reaching Boston with but eleven dollars. He entered Andover Seminary, where he studied fiercely, learning Greek, Hebrew, Chaldee, Syriac, Arabic, Samaritan, Rabbinic, Persian, Turkish,

and Spanish, and often studying fourteen and sixteen
hours a day.   He was a fine flute-player, and when he
sold his flute the students bought it back
for him.   He managed to support himself
by working in wood.

Sent out in 1831 by the American
Board, he labored most zealously for
the Spanish Jews in Constantinople, descendants of those driven from Spain,
and translated the entire Bible into their
Hebrew-Spanish tongue.   In his later years, with the
ardor of youth, he turned to work for the Moslems, and
translated the Bible into Osmanli-Turkish, the language
of the educated Turks.   During all this his evangelistic
labors were eager and powerful.   They were also most
varied, for he could speak in ten languages and read as
many more.

SCHAUFFLER

THE AMERICAN BOARD, which has practically to itself
the mission field of Turkey, with the exception of Syria,
divides its work into four sections.   The European Turkey
Mission labors in Bulgaria and Macedonia, where it began
work in 1858.   This mission works south of the Balkans,
while the mission of the Northern Methodists, founded
one year earlier, occupies the region north.   The political
ferment of the region and the misgovernment or no government of the Turks have greatly hindered the work.
William W. Merriam of the American Board was slain
by brigands in 1862, and his wife, who was with him,
died from the shock.   Terrible Turkish massacres and
cruel persecutions have been frequent.

MISS ELLEN M. STONE, missionary of the American
Board in Salonica, the ancient Thessalonica in Mace-

donia, went out in 1878. She became an experienced and greatly beloved teacher of Bulgarian teachers and Bible women, for whom she had been holding a summer school in Bansko, and was returning from it when, on September 3, 1901, she was captured, with a devoted native assistant, Katharine S. Tsilka. The Macedonian brigands held them in captivity for 172 days, and released them only on payment of $68,200 in gold, raised by popular subscription in the United States. Madame Tsilka's girl baby was born during this captivity. The entire affair, so full of harrowing details, brought home to the Christian world the dangers under which missionaries pursue their work in these unquiet lands.

AT CONSTANTINOPLE steady labors have been maintained since 1831 by the American Board, the chief work being among the Armenians. The first Armenian church was formed in 1846. It was at Constantinople that **ELIAS RIGGS**, who went to Greece as a missionary in 1833, accomplished most of his prodigious labors. He died in 1901, at the age of ninety, having been an active missionary for seventy years. As a writer of hymns, a journalist, and a commentator, he was fruitful, but his most conspicuous service was the aid he gave in the translation of the Bible into Turkish, and his unaided translation of the Bible into Armenian and Bulgarian.

HAMLIN

CYRUS HAMLIN was another famous missionary at Constantinople. He was a typical Yankee, able to turn his hand successfully to all sorts of mechanical work, battling in boyhood against grim poverty, resourceful all his life in the face of innumerable difficulties.

Setting out for Turkey in 1838, he made his lathe and his self-made chemical and physical apparatus most efficient evangelistic aids.   He started workshops to manufacture clothing for his pupils, and to make stove-pipe and stoves, and during the Crimean War set up an immense bakery which supplied the British soldiers with 14,000 pounds of bread a day.   He was the founder and first president of that splendid Christian institution, Robert College, into the building of whose walls he put all of his loving skill.

IN ASIATIC TURKEY the work of the American Board is divided into three missions, — the Western, from the Black Sea to the Mediterranean; the Central, in ancient Cilicia, north of Syria; and the Eastern, in Armenia and Mesopotamia, along the upper reaches of the Tigris and Euphrates.   The principal work is for the Armenians, and it has been richly blessed.   Three important colleges are conducted by these missions — Euphrates College at Harpoot, Central Turkey College at Aintab, and Anatolia College at Marsovan, besides a large number of girls' colleges, prominent among them being the American College for Girls at Constantinople.   As a basis for this higher education, a large number of boarding-schools, industrial schools, and more than three hundred primary schools are conducted by the missions.   While the Armenians are chiefly reached, the Greeks, Kurds, Syrians, and Turks are also influenced.

THE ARMENIAN MASSACRES are the most momentous event in the history of the mission to Turkey.   They began in the Sassoun district in the eastern part of Asiatic Turkey in August, 1894, and they raged for two years. They were instigated directly by the Sultan, whose own mother was an Armenian woman. He made use of the Turkish troops and of the fierce Kurdish tribes.

Amid circumstances of the most outrageous cruelty, more than 40,000 Armenian Christians were slain — the flower of the country. They were burned alive. They were tortured in all the ways an inhuman soldiery could devise. Children were placed in a row that it might be seen how many could be killed by a single bullet. A hundred women were shut up in a church, and after the Turks had satiated their lust upon them, they were dispatched with the sword and bayonet. Thousands of women were forcibly taken to a life-in-death in Turkish harems. Their towns were burned, their fields laid waste. About forty thousand were compelled to accept Mohammedanism, but most of them preferred death. Four hundred thousand persons were left destitute, and the enormous task of providing for their needs and of caring for their defenceless orphans taxed to its utmost the resources of Christian philanthropy.

Mission property was burned at Marash and at Euphrates College, but no missionary was killed. The most exalted heroism was shown by the native Christians and by the missionaries. Especially conspicuous was the noble work of some of the women missionaries, such as that of Corinna Shattuck, facing the mob alone at Urfa and protecting the natives from them, or that of Dr. Grace Kimball at Van, organizing a splendid system of relief work that was the salvation of thousands of lives.

IX

ARABIA

ARABIA is one-third as large as all Europe, and larger than all the United States east of the Mississippi. The population, however, is only about eight million — a little more than twice that of the city of New York.

The land lies in three rings. The coast ring consists of " Arabia Petræa," or stony Arabia, in the northwest with the Sinai country, together with "Arabia Felix," "Araby the Blest," the fertile west and south coasts. The remainder, " Arabia Deserta," is in two rings — a central plateau, the stronghold of the nation, from which come the beautiful horses, surrounded by the famous deserts where the wild Bedouins roam.

Missions in Arabia.

R A — Reformed Church in America.

In the coast ring are Mecca, the holy city of the Moslems, to which flock their pilgrims, 100,000 a year; Mocha, home of the renowned coffee; Muscat, home of the raisin; and the pearl fisheries along the Persian Gulf. Turkey exercises authority over the northwest, and Great Britain owns Aden, but the greater part of the country is made up of independent provinces. Arabia is especially worthy of missionary effort, not only because it is the religious centre of Mohammedanism, but also because the Arabs are a noble race, of fine physique and superior intellect, measurably free from superstition and tolerant of other faiths.

RAYMUND LULL was the first Christian missionary to the Moslems. He was a young nobleman, born in 1236 in the island of Majorca, and at the age of thirty was suddenly turned to Christ from a life of sensuality. He sold his property, provided for wife and children, and became a travelling herald of the Cross. He bought a Saracen slave, and learned Arabic from him, preaching first among the Mohammedans in Tunis, where he was imprisoned and condemned to death, but afterwards banished. He spent his life in most varied travels, striving to convert men through a quaint system of Christian philosophy, which rendered him famous but had little convincing power. At last, in poverty and great age, being nearly eighty, he again began preaching to the Saracens of northern Africa, who stoned him to death at Buggia in 1315.

SABAT and **ABDULLAH** were the first of the modern Arabs to become Christians. They were of distinguished family, visited Mecca, and then set out to see the world. They went first to Cabul, where Abdullah, taught by an Armenian, became a Christian, and fled at once to Bokhara. Sabat met his friend there and pitilessly delivered him up.

Abdullah was offered his life if he would abjure Christianity. He refused. One hand was cut off. Still he refused. The other hand was cut off. Still he held to Christ, and quietly bowed his head for the death stroke.

Filled with remorse, Sabat wandered to India, where he fell in with a copy of the Arabic New Testament, compared it with the Koran, became a Christian, and was baptized under the name of Nathaniel. When his brother in Arabia learned of this, he travelled in disguise, stole into Sabat's house, and wounded him with a dagger. Sabat sent him home with gifts to his mother, and himself became assistant to Henry Martyn, aiding him in his Persian translations.

Martyn, himself, on his way to Persia, stopped at Muscat, and intended, had his life been spared, to return to Arabia to perfect his translation of the New Testament.

ION GRANT NEVILLE KEITH FALCONER, the third son of the Earl of Kintore, was born in Scotland in 1856.

He was a vigorous youth, at twenty being president of the London Bicycle Club, and at twenty-two the champion British runner. He was an enthusiast in shorthand, and wrote the article on that subject for the Encyclopædia Britannica.

KEITH FALCONER

He became a notable Hebrew scholar, writing postal cards in that language to his teacher on all sorts of subjects, and taking highest Hebrew honors at Cambridge. After graduation he fell in love with Arabic, going to Egypt to study it, and becoming professor of it at Cambridge University.

He became interested in missions in Arabia, and, visiting Aden in 1885, determined at his own expense to conduct a mission in that neglected land. His purpose was to establish at Sheikh Othman, near Aden, a medical mission school and an industrial orphanage, which should become a starting-point for the interior.

At the end of 1886, with **DR. STEWART COWEN,** Falconer reached his field, going out as a Free Church missionary, though paying all expenses for himself and his young wife, his colleague and the buildings. He could not rent a stone house, but had to take a native hut. At once he began touring inland, and preaching every day. Immediately fevers seized upon his party, attacking even his vigorous frame. Seven attacks followed one after another, until, on May 10, 1887, quite suddenly he passed away, at the age of forty. His life, however, was not in vain, for his church continues his mission, a famous hospital has grown up and a school for boys, while the story of Keith Falconer's heroism has been a stimulus to the cause of missions everywhere.

THOMAS VALPY FRENCH served in India for forty years under the Church Missionary Society, becoming the first Bishop of Lahore. He was supremely consecrated to his holy calling, insisting that a Christian missionary should always go on foot, and refusing all but the most ordinary furniture for his house.

When an old man, he read Alexander Mackay's appeal for missionaries to go to Arabia and stop the African slave trade by transforming its promoters, the Arabs. As no one else responded, he resigned his bishopric, learned Arabic, and went all alone to Muscat, where he began most zealous labors for the Moslems. He was there, however, only

FRENCH

three months before a sunstroke in that terrible climate translated him, at the age of sixty-six, in the year 1891.

THE REFORMED CHURCH IN AMERICA is conducting the only American mission in Arabia, with three stations along the eastern coast. Students in their theological seminary at New Brunswick, N. J., took the initiative, and two of them, **JAMES CANTINE** and **SAMUEL M. ZWEMER**, became the pioneer missionaries, beginning their work at Busrah in 1891.

The mission has suffered much from sickness and persecution. Very early **KAMIL ABDEL MESSIAH** ("Servant of Christ"), their faithful Moslem assistant, was taken away, probably slain by poison. Attacks of Bedouins, arrests by fanatical Turks, and the early death of the noble young men, **PETER ZWEMER** and **GEORGE STONE**, have been great trials. Still the mission labors zealously, true to its motto, "O that Ishmael might live before Thee!"

X.

CHINA

THE PROBLEM IN CHINA is this. An empire of four and a quarter million square miles — one-sixth larger than the United States. A population of about four hundred million — five times that of the United States. A language the most difficult of all languages to learn. The people immersed in superstition, manacled to the past, and with a religion — Confucianism — which is merely a system of morality, unable, therefore, to make its professors moral. About twenty-eight hundred missionaries, including their wives and lay workers from abroad — one to 144,000 Chinese, while in the United States there is one minister to each 500 of the population. Yet, on the other side, there have been gathered under the banner of the Cross some 112,000 Chinese Protestant Christians, as faithful and true as any body of Christians the world has ever known — tested, many of them, by a persecution as bitter as the world has ever seen.

THE FOUR PERIODS OF MISSIONS in China are shown in the diagram. The Nestorians, a Christian sect of Syria and Persia, had flourishing missions in China during three centuries, from 500 A. D. Moved by the travels of Marco Polo, the Catholics made a missionary attempt under John Corvino, which endured for a century. The Jesuits, inspired by the great missionary, Xavier, came later, flourished for a century and a half, and then were banished, and many of their converts exiled. Then, in 1807, Robert Morrison introduced the present era of Protestant missions, which has progressed alongside of the Catholic missions.

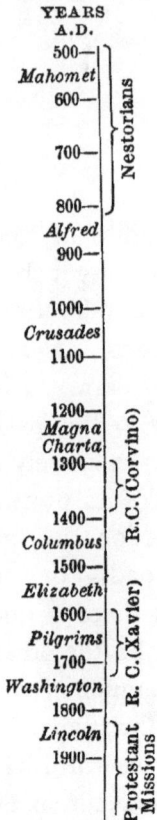

THE CENTURY OF PROTESTANT MISSIONS which is now closing is exhibited by another diagram. On the left are shown the dates when missions were established in the countries thus far studied. On the right are shown the dates when the principal missionaries began their work, either in China or in neighboring countries looking toward China.

The opium war, waged by England with the result of forcing the Chinese to permit the introduction of opium from India, had at least one good result — it opened to foreign occupancy the five "treaty ports," Canton, Amoy, Foochow, Ningpo, and Shanghai. The map shows how these became the centres of missionary operations.

Missionary work was at a standstill during the Tai-Ping rebellion against the Manchu dynasty, led by a Chinaman who claimed to be a Christian, and put down by the American, Frederic Ward, and the English general, "Chinese" Gordon.

The "Arrow War" with England was caused by the Chinese seizure of a ship, the "Arrow," flying the English flag. It ended in a treaty which granted toleration

Diagram (left margin):

YEARS A.D.
500— Mahomet
600—
700—
800— Alfred
900—
1000— Crusades
1100—
1200— Magna Charta
1300—
1400— Columbus
1500— Elizabeth
1600— Pilgrims
1700— Washington
1800— Lincoln
1900—

Nestorians
R. C. (Corvino)
R. C. (Xavier)
Protestant Missions

THE FOUR MISSION PERIODS IN CHINA.

to Christianity, and permitted foreign ministers to reside at Peking.

The Tientsin massacre of twenty French and Russians was caused by hostility to the Catholics, and half the slain were sisters of charity. The Catholic cathedral and orphanage were destroyed.

THE BOXER MASSACRES, the latest interruption to Chinese missions, were the most terrible event in the missionary history of the world. The causes began with the great wrong of the Opium War of 1841-2; but the recent causes were the humiliation of the defeat by Japan, the twenty-seven reform edicts of the Emperor seeking to change the Six Boards and the literary examinations, and to establish a modern army and a free

Carey. 1793— (India).	
	—1807. Morrison.
Judson. 1813— (Burma).	—1813. Milne.
Fisk. 1819— (Syria).	—1816. Medhurst.
	—1826. Gutzlaff.
Gutzlaff. 1828— (Siam).	
	—1830. Bridgman. Abeel.
Goodell. 1831— (Turkey).	
Perkins. 1833— (Persia).	—1833. Williams.
	—1834. Parker.
	—1837. Boone.
	—1841. *Opium War.*
	—1842. Lowrie. *Treaty Ports.*
	—1847. Collins. Burns.
	—1850. *Tai-Ping Rebellion.*
	—1853. Taylor. Nevius.
	—1855. John.
	—1856. *Arrow War.*
	—1858. *Toleration Treaty.*
	—1870. Gilmour. *Tientsin Massacre.*
	—1871. Murray.
	—1872. Mackay.
	—1875. Mackenzie.
Falconer. 1886— (Arabia).	
	—1900. *Boxer Massacres.*

press; the prompt suppression of the Emperor by the Empress Dowager; the Chinese hatred of railroads, those destroyers of cemeteries, some three thousand miles of which were building or being planned; the rise of the secret society known as the Boxers — though boxing had small place in their gatherings — which circulated still more widely than before the most absurd charges against the missionaries, to the effect that they poisoned wells, tore out the eyes of young children for medicine, and the like.

The outbreak came at the end of 1899. The Empress Dowager had ordered the extermination of all Christians, and that all foreigners should be driven from the land. Her commands were disobeyed at the south, but took effect at the north.

The calamity that came closest to American Christians was the tragedy of Pao-ting-fu, on June 30 and July 1, 1900, when the Presbyterian and Congregational missionaries were burnt alive, shot, stabbed, and beheaded — fifteen souls.

The greatest loss of missionary life, however, was in the province of Shansi and over the Mongolian border, where, by the fiendish governor, Yü Hsien, 113 missionaries with 46 of their children were murdered under all circumstances of barbarity.

Altogether, during those fearful months, 135 adult missionaries were killed and 53 children, 100 of these being British, 56 Swedish, and 32 from the United States. Nearly half of these belonged to the China Inland Mission. Perhaps fifty Catholic missionaries were also slain, together with 20,000 or 25,000 native Catholics. At least 5,000 native Protestants were butchered, exhibiting such heroism that sometimes the Boxers tore out their hearts to learn, if possible, where they got such courage.

At Peking the German minister, Baron von Ketteler, was assassinated in the street by the Chinese troops. At the British Legation more than four hundred foreigners, of eight nationalities, with three hundred and fifty Chinese, stood a siege of eight weeks, being confronted sometimes with as many as 10,000 men armed with modern weapons. Four officers and forty-four men were killed or died of wounds, but the great majority were wonderfully preserved. The Methodist missionary, Rev. F. D. Gamewell, had charge of the fortifications.

After the capture of the Taku forts and the siege and capture of Tientsin, followed by a long and perilous march, the allied troops — Russian, British, German, American, Japanese, Italian, French, and Austrian — entered Peking on August 14, 1900, the Empress Dowager escaping by flight.

These stirring events have proved the stanchness of Chinese Christianity; and already in China, as elsewhere in the world's history, the blood of the martyrs has become the seed of the church.

ROBERT MORRISON, the son of a Scotch maker of lasts and boot-trees, born in 1782, became in 1807 the first Protestant missionary to China. While only thirteen he was able to repeat the whole of the 119th Psalm. He worked from twelve to fourteen hours a day, but he kept his book open before him, and even moved his bed into his workshop so that he might study late at night. He early formed the desire to be a missionary, and to go where the difficulties were the greatest. He had his desire. Compelled by the hostility of the East

MORRISON

India Company to go out by way of New York, it was there, when the ship owner asked him sneeringly, "Do you really expect to make an impression on the idolatry of the great Chinese empire?" that Morrison made his famous answer: "No, sir; I expect that God will." At first, for fear of the hostile Chinese of Canton, Morrison wore Chinese clothes and ventured out only rarely and at night. He studied incessantly, and lived with such economy that at one time he could scarcely walk across the room. Finally, his safety and support were assured by his appointment as translator to the East India Company, at a salary of $2,500 a year. He labored for twenty-seven years in China, doing pioneer work of the highest importance, translating the Bible, and preparing a great dictionary of the language, as well as a grammar. The first Chinese convert was Tsai-A-Ko, baptized in 1814, after Morrison had labored for seven disheartening years. In all, the great missionary won only ten converts; but they were, as he prayed they might be, "the first-fruits of a great harvest."

WILLIAM MILNE, a poor Scotch shepherd boy, became the second Protestant missionary to China. In his early youth he was wild, "a very deevil for swearing," as his neighbors said. But he became converted, and at the age of twenty determined to be a foreign missionary. Very dutifully he then spent five years in securing a support for his aged mother and his sisters. The committee of ministers who examined him as a missionary candidate thought he "would not do," and proposed that he go out as a mechanic. Milne promptly answered: "Anything, anything — if only engaged in the work." But at last they decided to accept him, and he joined Morrison in 1813.

He studied Chinese in Canton, and ultimately became a notable scholar. Within ten years (for his service was no longer than that — he died at the age of thirty-seven), he had thoroughly studied conditions in the East Indies, and, since he was not permitted to live in Canton, had established a missionary station at Malacca in the Malay Peninsula, started a free school for the Chinese, a college, and periodicals in both Chinese and English, besides sharing with Morrison the honor of giving the entire Bible to China. His first convert, Leang-Afa, was the first ordained Chinese evangelist. So much for the man who " would not do."

WALTER HENRY MEDHURST, an Englishman, was the third Protestant missionary to China (notice that the names of the first three missionaries to China begin with M), sailing for Malacca in 1816. He was a printer missionary, and had charge of the Shanghai mission press, the pioneer in that work. He was largely responsible for the great revision of the Chinese Bible made in the middle of the century. For Dr. Medhurst was far more than a printer; he was a remarkable linguist, able to speak and write in eight or nine languages. Many attempts were made to entice his conspicuous abilities into worldly pursuits, but always in vain. He was a preacher missionary also, and went many times into the interior of China, where he fearlessly proclaimed the gospel, though at the peril of his life.

KARL GUTZLAFF, a poor German apprentice to a saddler, found himself, at the age of eighteen, longing to be a missionary. He expressed his longings in a sonnet addressed to the King of Prussia, and this procured for him an education in view of his life work. He became a physician, and his learning and medical skill added greatly to his missionary power. Obtaining a government post in China, he carried on his missionary work at his own expense, and, except at the beginning, independent of all missionary societies. He became interested in Bible translation, and aided Medhurst in his revision of the Chinese Bible. Personally, he was most daring in his preaching, making three missionary voyages along GUTZLAFF the coast of China, once in the disguise of a Chinaman. It was his crusade in Europe on behalf of missions in China that led to the founding of the China Inland Mission and the great work of J. Hudson Taylor. Gützlaff died in 1851, at the early age of forty-eight.

DAVID ABEEL, a young medical student, became converted and was led into the ministry. While at the theological seminary, he prepared a special place for prayer in a forest near by. He was very faithful, and an inmate of his family said that he never sat with them or even passed through the rooms without making some remarks of a religious character. Very naturally he and Mr. Bridgman became the first American missionaries to the Flowery Kingdom, setting sail in 1829. His always feeble health forced him to become a travelling missionary, and he spent most of his time in missionary jour-ABEEL neys among the East Indies, and rousing to the needs of missions in China the Christians of Europe and America; nevertheless, he founded the Amoy Mission, now conducted by the Reformed Church in America, of which

he was a member, although a missionary of the American Board. As this sainted man, worn out by his labors, came home to die, at the early age of forty-two, he wrote that it was doubtful "*which home he should reach first.*"

ELIJAH C. BRIDGMAN, under appointment from the American Board, sailed for China with Mr. Abeel, and spent his first year at Canton teaching English to two Chinese lads, learning Chinese, and preaching in defiance of the edict of the government. He became the first editor of that great aid to missions, *The Chinese Repository*, and edited it for twenty years. He labored successfully as an evangelist at Canton and Shanghai,

BRIDGMAN

founding the mission in the latter place, but his chief work was the translation of the Scriptures. His thirty-two useful years in China came to an end in 1861. On his death-bed his one anxiety was expressed in these words: "Will the churches come up to the work?"

SAMUEL WELLS WILLIAMS, who followed Drs. Abeel and Bridgman to China in 1833, succeeded the latter in the editorship of *The Chinese Repository*, with which he also was connected for twenty years. His labors, chiefly in Canton, were most fruitful along literary lines, and especially in the production of that valuable work, "The Middle Kingdom." In addition, however, he served as secretary of legation in Japan and at Peking, and was Commodore Perry's interpreter on his famous entry of Japan, which was the first step toward opening that country to missionary labors.

Williams learned Japanese from seven shipwrecked seamen whom he and Gützlaff endeavored to carry back to

Japan, but the batteries of two ports fired upon them and compelled them to return to Canton. He took some of the sailors into his own house, translated for them Genesis and Matthew, and converted them to Christianity.

In 1860 Dr. Williams with Dr. Ashmore, the eminent Baptist missionary, were crossing the Pacific as the only passengers. There were about four hundred Chinese between decks, whom the captain thought it necessary to put on short allowance of food. They rebelled, coming aft in a great crowd and brandishing clubs in his face. It was necessary at last for the two missionaries to take command of the ship till they had settled the matter.

This learned and successful missionary died in 1884.

PETER PARKER, sent out by the American Board in 1834, was the practical founder of medical missions. " He opened China to the gospel," it was said, " at the point of his lancet." He established a free hospital in Canton, an eye infirmary, and a medical missionary society, and began the great work of training native physicians and surgeons. Howqua, the leading merchant, gave him for years the free use of his building, though he suspiciously sent one of his clerks to keep an eye on all proceedings!

WILLIAM J. BOONE, M. D., who sailed from America in 1837, became the first Episcopal bishop of China, and translated the Prayer Book into Chinese. He was aided by a noble wife, who on her death-bed said with her last breath, " If there is a mercy in life for which I feel thankful, it is that God has condescended to call me to be a missionary."

WALTER LOWRIE was converted in a college revival, and promptly determined to be a foreign missionary. He desired, as he said, a post " in western Africa, the white man's grave," but the Presbyterian Board sent him to China. He sailed in 1842. He closes his journal of the voyage with these words, which he often repeated as if in sad prophecy: " What a blessed place heaven will be, *where there is no more sea!* " Required to go to Singapore, he was driven for fifty-three days by a monsoon up and down the China Sea, and finally into

LOWRIE

Manila. Proceeding, the ship was wrecked four hundred miles from land, and for five days the passengers suffered much in a small, leaky boat driven by a severe gale. On another occasion the rudder of his ship gave way, and left it at the mercy of the waves. Finally, after a few years of earnest and most successful labors at Ningpo, he died upon the sea between Shanghai and Ningpo, at the hands of Chinese pirates. While these pirates were maiming the sailors and ransacking the vessel, he was calmly sitting at the bow, reading a pocket Bible which he had saved with great difficulty on the occasion of his shipwreck. Three men seized him as he was reading, and threw him into the sea.

JUDSON DWIGHT COLLINS, pioneer Methodist missionary to China, was a very young man when he begged Bishop Janes to be sent to China to open a mission there. " Engage me a place before the mast," he said, " and my own strong arm will pull me to China and support me while there." He went to Foochow, because it was the only port unoccupied by Protestants. He lived on an island, and it was months before he could gain a foothold in the city itself. It was in this mission, in 1848, that the first Sunday school in China was held. In five years the strength of the heroic young missionary gave out, and he was compelled to return to America, only to die in his thirtieth year.

BURNS

WILLIAM C. BURNS was an earnest Scotch evangelist. He labored faithfully in his own country and in Canada. He depended upon the free-will offerings of the French Canadians, and if they gave him more than he needed, he spent the remainder in charity. He became the first missionary to China of the English Presbyterians, going out in 1847. For twenty years he travelled up and down the Chinese empire, dressing as a Chinaman, living on the merest necessaries, suffering all manner of hardships, now robbed and stripped of everything, now lying sick, lonely, and uncared-for. He gave the Chinese " The Pilgrim's Progress " and a popular hymn-book, and everywhere preached with great fervor and power. His death was due to a journey of especial difficulty in Manchuria.

J. HUDSON TAYLOR

J. HUDSON TAYLOR often travelled with Mr. Burns, and the spirit and methods of the two men were identical. Mr. Taylor is the founder of the China Inland Mission, that largest of all missionary bodies in China, and has been its guiding spirit from the beginning in 1865. In that year eleven out of the eighteen provinces in China were entirely destitute of missionary work. In all these provinces the China Inland Mission is now laboring. Its missionaries go without any stipulated salary, trusting to God for their support. Numbers of them are supported by themselves or by special friends.

JOHN LIVINGSTON NEVIUS was one of the best rounded of missionaries. He spent nearly forty years in China under the Presbyterian Board North, setting forth in 1853. Laboring first at Ningpo, with his courageous wife he opened a mission in Hangchow, the two taking up their abode in an old Taoist temple. They were compelled to leave just before the occupation of Hangchow by the Tai-Ping insurrectionists, in the

NEVIUS

course of which twenty thousand Chinese were massacred; their temple with all their belongings was destroyed.

The greater part of Mr. Nevius' service was given to the northern province of Shantung, where Confucius and his distinguished pupil, Mencius, were born. From Tung-chow in turn they were compelled to flee just before the Tientsin massacre of 1870. At Chefoo the missionaries passed through two famines, in one of which Dr. Nevius gave efficient aid to 383 starving villages, sleeping in a room with huge sacks of relief money. His work in Shantung was formed on the basis of self-support, in which he trained the natives so far as possible, becoming influential in planting that great principle in Japan, India, Siam, and especially in Korea.

GRIFFITH JOHN, a Welshman, was sent to Shanghai in 1855 by the London Society. The rebellion of the Tai-Ping chief, Hungsewtsuen, was in full progress. This able man was a nominal Christian, and had had instruction from an American missionary. The centre of his revolt was Nanking, which he held against the forces of the government from 1853 to 1864. In the midst of many strange experiences, Mr. John visited the rebel chieftain and obtained from him an edict of religious toleration.

Another of Mr. John's important journeys was to Hankow, the great interior city, which he opened to the gospel in 1861. His journey of 1868 to Chung-tu, capital of the extreme western province of Sz-

GRIFFITH JOHN chuen — a distance of 3,000 miles — was the most extensive missionary journey that had been made in the Celestial Empire. But Mr. John's great work has been literary. He translated the Old Testament into " easy Wen-li," and millions of copies of his various writings have been distributed.

WILLIAM MURRAY is the great missionary to the multitude of China's blind. He was a simple Scotch postman, who studied Hebrew during one-third of his long routes, the Greek Testament during another third, and spent the remaining third in prayer that he might become a foreign missionary. During sixteen years of colportage work in China, he was seized with a great pity for the half million of poor blind men in that sad empire. One day, after long study, there came to him the vision of a wonderful system of characters by which a blind lad can learn to read and write that difficult language in six weeks.

JAMES GILMOUR, the apostle to Mongolia, was the son of a Scotch carpenter, a spirited lad and brilliant scholar. His determination was shown in his student days when some intoxicating liquor was put in his room. He poured it out of the window, saying, " Better on God's earth than in His image." He went to Peking the year of the

Tientsin massacre, and proceeded at once to his chosen
field among the rude nomads of Mongolia.   Here, in terrible loneliness yet with no privacy, living
in tents amid all kinds of discomforts,
Gilmour toiled for twenty years, dying,
worn-out, in 1891.   One brief interval
of joyful romance was his marriage to
Emily Prankard, a beautiful and heroic
Englishwoman, to whom Gilmour made a
proposal of marriage without having seen

GILMOUR

her, and who thereupon went out to China without having
seen him.   Her splendid sharing of her husband's tent-
life among the Mongolians, and her untimely death, make
up one of the most lovely chapters of missionary history.
To his two boys, being educated in England, he wrote
the most tender letters, never using blotting-paper, but
always kneeling to pray for them while the ink dried ;
and their boyish replies he always carried with him.

GEORGE LESLIE MACKAY is the great missionary of the
Presbyterian Church in Canada.   His marvellous work
covered with Christian influences the entire
northern part of the great island of Formosa, which now, as a result of the China-
Japan War, has been ceded to Japan.   Dr.
Mackay married a Chinese lady, who aided
him wonderfully in winning the Chinese
women.   He obtained his success chiefly
through the use of native converts, sending
them forth as soon as possible to preach
the gospel to other Chinese.

GEORGE L.
MACKAY

J. KENNETH MACKENZIE is the medical missionary of
the London Society who attended in her sickness the wife

of the great viceroy, Li Hung Chang, and thus won his powerful favor for medical missions and for Christianity. This interest of the viceroy's grew into an important hospital with a female department, a medical school, and a medical staff for the Chinese army and navy. This beloved and skilful doctor was also an untiring evangelist. Beginning his work in 1875 at Hankow with Griffith John,

MACKENZIE   he spent his first Sunday boarding steamers and inviting sailors to the meetings on shore. For the opium habit alone he treated in one year 700 persons. On his removal in 1879 to Tientsin, Li Hung Chang set apart for his dispensary an entire quadrángle in one of the finest temples. Through Mackenzie's labors the Chinese began to build and support their own hospitals; and always, in the hospital placed in his charge, the missionary promoted "the Double Cure" — soul with body. His sudden death from smallpox, on Easter, 1888, was greatly deplored.

THE PRESENT DISPOSITION of mission forces in China is indicated, for the leading American boards, upon the map. *The Congregationalists* have four missions : South China (Hong-Kong and Canton), Foochow, North China, and Shansi. The last two suffered fearfully in the Boxer massacres. *The Presbyterians* labor in seven missions : Canton (where Dr. John G. Kerr spent his glorious forty-seven years as one of the world's greatest medical missionaries) ; Central China (Ningpo, Shanghai, etc., with the important mission press at Shanghai); the island of Hainan on the southeast; the inland province of Hunan ; Peking, and two missions in Shantung. *The*

Boards and Missionaries
IN CHINA

Northern Methodists are working at Foochow, and inland in Fuhkien; at Nanking in Kiangsu; in Shantung and Peking; and in Szchuen province of West China. *The Northern Baptists* have missions in South China, the oldest being at Swatow, where the veteran Dr. William Ashmore has toiled so long and ably; in East China (Ningpo and vicinity); in Central China (Hupeh province); and in West China (Szchuen province). *The Southern Presbyterian* missions begin at Hangchow, and

extend northward through Kiangsu along the Grand
Canal. *The Southern Methodists* labor at Shanghai and
the region around, where also the *Southern Baptists* work,
the other fields of the latter denomination centering at
Canton in the south and Shantung province in the
north. *The Canadian Presbyterians*, in addition to their
famous work in Formosa, are at work in Shanghai,
Macao, and the inland province of Honan. *The Canadian
Methodists* have two stations in the western frontier province, Szchuen. The work of the *Reformed Church in
America* is grouped around Amoy, where Dr. Abeel
founded the mission in 1842, and where Mr. Pohlman
erected probably the first church building in China for
Chinese worshippers only. The remaining American
missions in China are those of the *Friends* in Nanking,
the *Episcopalians* in Shanghai and Hankow, the *Christian
and Missionary Alliance* in the south (centering at Macao)
and in Central China (Wuhu), the *Seventh Day Baptists*
in Shanghai, the *Cumberland Presbyterians* in Hunan, and
the *Disciples of Christ* in Nanking, Shanghai, and the
regions around.

XI.

KOREA

KOREA, "the Land of the Morning Calm," has an area of 84,000 square miles, about the area of Minnesota or Kansas. The population, however, is about twelve million, equal to the combined population of New York and Illinois.

It is an agricultural country, with mineral resources little developed. Castes are almost as numerous as in India. The people are largely Confucians, worshippers of ancestors and of demons. The shamans, or devil doctors, are numbered by the thousand, and wield a terrible influence.

CATHOLIC MISSIONS in Korea have a history full of splendid deeds. "The Hermit Land" first received the light of Christianity, though a dim reflection only, through a Korean student named Stonewall, who chanced to meet, in 1777, some Jesuit books in the Chinese language. The new truths spread, and a strange church was formed merely from books. This infant church refused to worship ancestors — a doctrine which led to bitter persecution and martyrdom.

Hearing of the groping Christians in Korea, the Catholic church in Peking attempted to send them teachers. The first to penetrate beyond the forbidden frontier was a young Chinese priest, Jacques Tsiu, who reached Seoul in 1794. The three Korean Christians who guided him

CATHOLIC MISSIONS IN KOREA.

—1777. Stonewall.
—1793. *Carey in India.*
—1794. Tsiu.

—1807. *Morrison in China.*

—1813. *Judson in Burma.*

—1819. *Fisk in Syria.*

—1828. *Gutzlaff in Siam.*
—1831. *Goodell in Turkey.*
—1833. *Perkins in Persia.*
—1835. Maibant.

—1845. Kim.

—1866. Catholics banished.

PROTESTANT MISSIONS

—1873. Ross.

—1884. Allen.
—1885. Underwood.
     Appenzeller.
—1886. *Falconer in Arabia.*

—1894. Chino-Japanese War.
—1896. Reid.
  MISSION HISTORY IN
     KOREA.

were seized, their knees crushed, their arms and legs dislocated, and when they refused to betray him, they were beheaded. Tsiu remained in hiding till 1801, and then, to prevent further persecution of his friends, he gave himself up, at the age of thirty-two, and was beheaded.

Still the church grew, and sent messages to the outer world beseeching instruction. The first French Catholic missionary to reach Seoul, Pierre Maibant, crawled under walls through water drains. That was in 1835. The next came in disguise as a Korean widower in mourning. In 1845 Andrew Kim, a Korean who knew absolutely nothing of navigation, brought a shapeless junk across the sea to Shanghai and carried back some French priests. He himself soon after suffered martyrdom. Terrible persecutions were bravely endured. One Korean Christian, sixty-one years old, after long torture was laid on the icy ground at night, and water thrown over his naked body till he was encased in a tomb of ice, where he died, still calling upon the name of Jesus. By 1861 there were said to be 18,000 Catholic Christians in the forbidden land, and they began to proclaim their religion more boldly. But in 1866, when pressure from foreign nations began to force the hermit nation open to the world, a fierce assault was made upon Christianity, all the foreign priests were slain or banished, and the same fate was meted out to thousands of native converts.

CHINA, the traditional overlord of Korea, at length, taught by its own bitter experience, advised the " Hermit Nation " no longer to struggle against the inevitable, but to throw open its doors to foreign commerce. The United States in 1882 was the first to seize this opportunity, and effected a treaty, other nations quickly following.

These treaties recognize Korea as a state independent of China, and when China in 1894 insisted upon her ancient sovereignty in Korea, the Chino-Japanese war followed, thoroughly proving the immense superiority of Japan's new western civilization, and thoroughly humiliating China. The result was the cession of Formosa to Japan, and the giving of a modern constitution to Korea. Under this new order Protestant Christianity is making rapid progress.

THE UNITED PRESBYTERIAN missionaries from Scotland, led by Dr. John Ross, and working from near-by Manchuria, began as early as 1873 to labor along the border of Korea, and Dr. Ross and Mr. Webster even penetrated the country at the north, risking their lives, and baptized eighty-five men.

DR. H. N. ALLEN, of the Northern Presbyterian Church, was the first Protestant missionary to reside in Korea, being sent there on the earnest invitation of a Korean

Christian named Rijutei in 1884. For his safety he was
made physician to the United States Legation. Soon
he had an opportunity to tend the wounds of Prince
Min Yong Ik, severely injured in an anti-Japanese revolt,
and by his skill, so superior to that of the native surgeons, whose wisest proposal was to pour wax into the
wounds, he won so great a reputation that the government placed him in charge of a hospital.

HORACE G. UNDERWOOD, D. D., a Northern Presbyterian, was the first Protestant minister to reach Korea.
He arrived in 1885, and performed the first baptism in
1886. He has become a great leader in the system of
self-supporting mission work for which Korea is now
noted. No Korean is thought fit for church-membership
unless he is vigorously engaged in propagating the gospel.
The strong churches send out from one to four home
missionaries. The people are required to build their
own churches with their own hands, and to pay for medi-
cines in the hospitals. Practically all the Protestant
churches in Korea — about two hundred — are self-supporting, and their members, out of their great poverty,
contribute to the work an average of more than $11 a
year. The converts come at the rate of a hundred a
month.

REV. H. G. APPENZELLER and William B. Scranton,
M. D., the first missionaries of the Northern Methodists,
reached Korea a short time after Dr. Underwood. They
began work at Seoul, and the school they established
received its name from the emperor himself: "Hall for
Rearing Useful Men." This institution is a power for
good throughout the kingdom. The Methodists have
also established a very influential publishing-house.

The Southern Methodists began work in 1896, their first missionary being C. F. Reid, D. D. They labor in the closest union with the Northern Methodists. The same fellowship is manifested by the four Presbyterian bodies — the Northern Presbyterians, the Australian Presbyterians, who arrived in 1889, the Southern Presbyterians, who sent out six missionaries in 1892, and the Nova Scotian Presbyterians, who began work in 1897. Korea is a fine example of missionary comity, and the work is not allowed to overlap.

XII.

JAPAN

JAPAN, Dai Nippon, " the Great Kingdom of the Ris-
ing Sun," is perhaps the most fascinating of mission fields.
The empire consists of five large islands and about two
thousand small ones, occupying a vast space measuring
nearly three thousand miles wide and two thousand miles
from north to south. The area, however, is only 150,000
square miles, less than that of California across the Pacific. The population is forty-four millions, not far from
that of Great Britain, which it also resembles in area,
enterprise, and naval destiny. These islands are volcanic,
the renowned Mt. Fuji being perhaps the most beautiful
mountain in the world. Japan is the earthquake centre
of the globe.

THE JAPANESE are a charming people, polite above
other nations, possessors of keen intellects, ardent patriots, and honorers of women. Their chief faults are
licentiousness, untruthfulness, dishonesty, and intemperance. The hairy race of Ainus at the north are different
in many ways, and are probably the survivors of an
aboriginal people. The Japanese language is one of the
most difficult on earth. Their religions are Shintoism,
the national faith, which is largely a worship of ancestors
and of the emperor; Confucianism, which has a more
healthful influence than in China; Buddhism, whose

American Missions in Japan.

BN—Baptists, North.
BS—Baptists, South.
C.—Congregational.
CA—Christian and Missionary Alliance.
CC—Christian Convention.
CP—Cumberland Presbyterian.
D—Disciples of Christ.
E—Episcopalian.
F—Friends.
FM—Free Methodists.
MC—Methodists of Canada.
MN—Methodists, North.
MP—Methodist Protestants.
MS—Methodists, South.
PC—Presbyterians of Canada.
PN—Presbyterians, North.
PS—Presbyterians, South.
RA—Reformed Church in America.
UB—United Brethren.

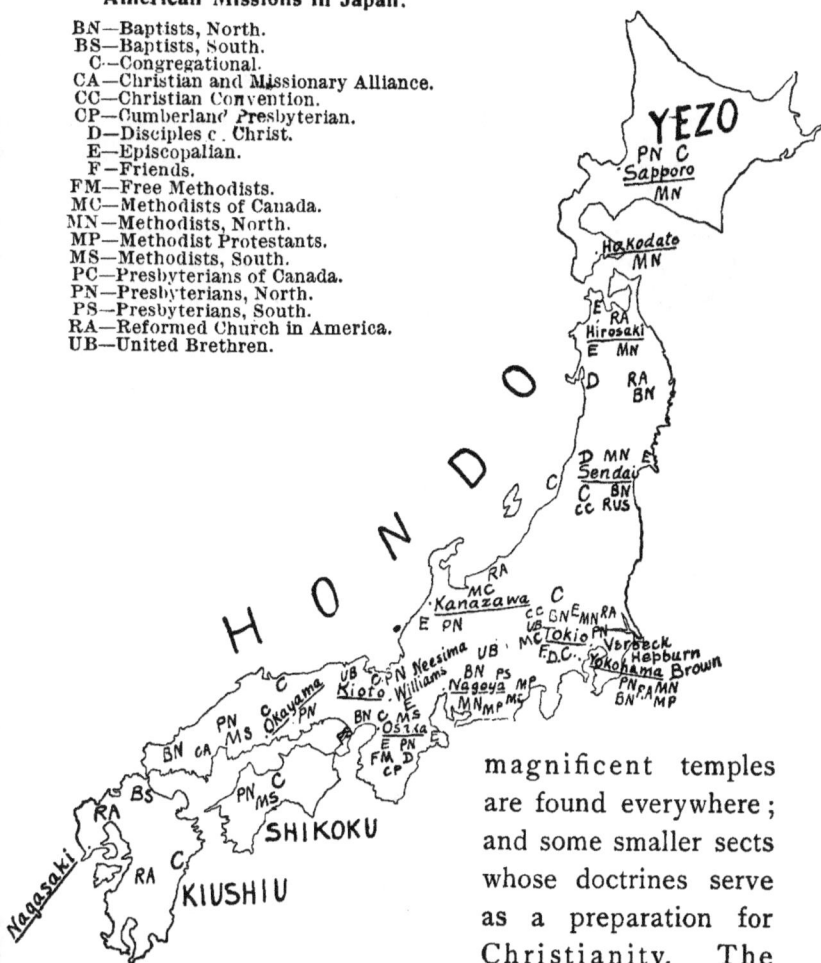

magnificent temples are found everywhere; and some smaller sects whose doctrines serve as a preparation for Christianity. The Ainus worship fetiches.

CATHOLIC MISSIONS in Japan were the last work of that able man, Francis Xavier. He reached Japan in 1549, ten years after the first European saw the country. Thinly clad and barefoot, in the depth of winter, he jour neyed through the snow to the capital. After laboring with measurable success for two and a half years, he turned toward China, and died in 1552 off the coast of that inhospitable shore.

The Jesuits rapidly grew in influence. They established a printing press and sent forth many books, but no Bibles. It is said that by 1613 there were two hundred missionaries and two million con-verts. Soon after that date, however, a terrible persecution arose, thousands of Christians were imprisoned, tortured, exiled, or beheaded. In 1637 they made a last stand in Kiushiu, withstood a siege of two months, and at last, with the surrender of 27,000 prisoners, the Roman Church ceased in Japan, and the country for two centuries was closed to Christianity.

XAVIER

The Dutch alone were permitted to live on a little island facing Nagasaki. They were not allowed to import Bibles or Christian books, and they could bring only one vessel a year from Europe. Japan-ese sailors, driven often out to sea and rescued by foreign ships, would not be received when the for-eigners humanely tried to land them upon their native shores.

Seven such waifs, reaching China, were sent back, together with the missionaries Gützlaff and Williams, but their ship was fired upon and not permitted to land. The two missionaries learned the Japanese language from the men thus providentially brought to them, and prepared portions of Scripture ready for Japan when it should throw open its doors. The treaty of Commodore Perry in 1854 and that of Townsend Harris in 1858 accom-plished this greatly desired result, and Yokohama and Nagasaki were opened to commerce and residence.

THE FIRST PROTESTANT MISSIONARIES to enter the new field were Episcopalians, Rev. John Liggins and Rev. C. M. Williams. The latter afterwards became the first Bishop of Japan. Only a few months later came the Presbyterian, J. C. Hepburn, M. D., LL. D., whose great work was the preparation of the first Japanese and English dictionary. He was also the chairman of the international committee for the translation of the Bible,

HEPBURN

— a work completed in 1880. It was Dr. Hepburn who preached the first American sermon in Japan, the occasion being the discovery by a company of curious visiting officials of a picture of the crucifixion which they insisted upon having explained.

It was in Dr. Hepburn's dispensary, in 1872, that the first church in Japan was organized. It consisted of nine young men and two older, all Japanese, and was called simply "The Church of Christ in Japan," refusing to accept any sectarian name.

Indeed, above all other mission fields, the history of Protestantism in Japan has been free from the rivalries and animosities of denominationalism. In 1877 the six Presbyterian denominations working in Japan united in one church, which thus forms a powerful Protestant organization. In a similar way the various Methodist bodies are united, and the Episcopalian bodies also, while a committee on co-operation is now looking toward a union of all missionary forces.

THE FIRST BAPTIST MISSIONARY to Japan was a seaman, Jonathan Goble, in Commodore Perry's expedition of 1854, who returned home, told his experiences, and in 1860 was sent out as the first Baptist missionary. Dr. Nathan Brown, who went out later, translated the New Testament into Japanese, having already performed the same service for the Assamese. Besides extensive missions in Japan proper, the Baptists carry on work in the Riukiu (Loochoo) Islands to the south.

GUIDO FRIDOLIN VERBECK, a most important factor in the founding of New Japan, was born in Holland in 1830. He was turned toward missions by Gützlaff and the Moravians, but first he had an experience as civil engineer in the western United States which was a great advantage to him in after years.

The influence of the Dutch and Americans in Japan made it most suitable that the pioneer missionary efforts should be

VERBECK

made by the Dutch Church in America (the Reformed Church in America, as it is now called), and Verbeck, "the Americanized Dutchman," was a most suitable pioneer. He set sail in 1859.

In the meantime a noble Japanese, Murata, whose title was Wakasa no Kami, in the course of his duties as guard of Nagasaki harbor, found floating on the water one night a little Dutch New Testament. What he learned of the beautiful contents filled him with so great longing to know more that he sent a man to China to procure a Chinese translation. When he heard of Verbeck's arrival, he sent his brother to learn about the Bible, and this brother, with one other young man, made up Verbeck's first class.

Placards all over Japan offered large rewards for information concerning those that might teach or study the prohibited religion. Murata and his brother and another relative were the first whom Verbeck baptized — in 1866, and they were the first Japanese converts to Protestantism.

Gradually a school of Japanese young men grew around Verbeck in Nagasaki, and afterward he became organizer of the Imperial University at Tokyo, receiving from the Emperor a badge of honor which saved his life at one time when he was assailed by a mob.

At first the missionaries had to grope after the language with no aids whatever. "I have found the future tense!" cried one of them one day in great excitement. Verbeck became a wonderful master of Japanese, and his translations were remarkable. His evangelistic labors, his long service of thirty-eight years, and his training of many of the most eminent men in modern Japan, won for him a mighty and glorious influence, and when he died, in 1898, the Emperor himself did honor to his memory.

SAMUEL ROBBINS BROWN was the son of a mother full of the missionary spirit, the author of the beautiful hymn, "I love to steal awhile away." A Yankee school-teacher, he became an educational pioneer in China. Within twelve days from his summons by the American Board, he obtained the consent of his betrothed, was married, gave up his teaching, and set sail, reaching Macao early in 1839. He took charge of the Morrison School at Hong Kong, the first Christian school in China. It was he, also, who first persuaded young men of China to go to the United States for an education.

BROWN

His wife's failing health compelled Dr. Brown to
return home in 1847, and while here he became a pioneer
in the higher education of women.   When nearly fifty,
under the Reformed Church in America, he took up
entirely new work in Japan, going out in 1859, a pioneer
missionary of his church.   Making his first home in a
Buddhist temple at Kanagawa, he became, through a service of two decades, an important factor in the making of
new Japan, founding a theological seminary in his own
house, aiding in translating the Bible, and inducing the
Japanese government to send young princes for education
to America.   "If I had a hundred lives," he often said,
"I would give them all for Japan."

JOSEPH HARDY NEESIMA was born in 1843 of Shin-
toist parents, his father being a teacher of penmanship.
A boy of fifteen, Neesima observed that
the gods did not eat the food placed before them, and henceforth refused to worship them.   One day at school he caught
sight of a Dutch warship, whose beautiful
proportions, contrasted with the clumsy
native junks, were his first lesson in west-

NEESIMA   ern civilization.   He came across Bridgman's Chinese account of the United States, and a few
books teaching Christianity.   God was revealed to him
as his heavenly Father.   He longed to know more of the
wonderful land across the seas.

Gaining permission to visit a seaport city in 1864, he
managed to get passage to Shanghai.   There he obtained
a place on the American ship *Wild Rover*, waiting on the
table, and being called "Joe" — a name he retained.

Arrived in Boston, he won the interest of the ship's

owner, the noble Alpheus Hardy,
whose name he added to his
own. Mr. Hardy put him through
Phillips Academy and Amherst
College. He showed such ability
that he visited Europe as assistant
to the Japanese commissioner of
education, and his reports became
the foundation of Japan's present
system of schools.

In 1874 the American Board
sent Neesima to Japan, and in
1875 he accomplished the ambi-
tion of his life through the opening of the Doshisha, the great
Christian college, which started
with eight pupils. He became its
president, and raised it to the
rank of a university. By ten years
the eight scholars had become
230.

His life was filled with self-
denying efforts for his beloved
country. "My heart burns for
Japan," he wrote, "and I cannot
check it." Worn out, he died
in 1890, his last words being,
"Peace — joy — heaven." A
building capable of holding 3,000
persons had to be erected for his
funeral. The procession was a
mile and a half long, and in it —
most significant of all — was a

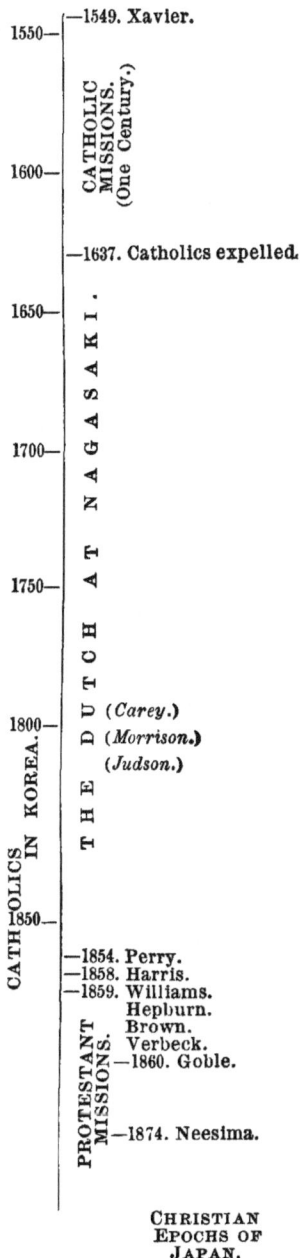

Timeline (right margin):

1549. Xavier.
CATHOLIC MISSIONS. (One Century.)
1637. Catholics expelled.
THE DUTCH AT NAGASAKI.
(Carey.)
(Morrison.)
(Judson.)
CATHOLICS IN KOREA.
1854. Perry.
1858. Harris.
1859. Williams. Hepburn. Brown. Verbeck.
1860. Goble.
PROTESTANT MISSIONS.
1874. Neesima.

CHRISTIAN EPOCHS OF JAPAN.

delegation of priests bearing a banner inscribed, "From the Buddhists of Osaka."

THE FIFTEEN YEARS, from 1873 when the edict boards forbidding the teaching of Christianity were removed and the whole force of missionaries was doubled, up to 1888, were marked by a rush of Japanese into the church; it seemed as if the empire would speedily become Christian. Then a severe reaction set in against everything foreign in its origin, and even hostility developed against the missionaries. After the war with China and foreign recognition of Japan as a world power, the tide began to turn, and again a great union evangelistic movement is sweeping men into the Kingdom by the thousand. The great part of the societies at work in Japan are from America — thirty-two in number. The chief centres of work are indicated on the map. No mission land is so well supplied with workers, and yet they are very inadequate to the vast need and the glorious opportunity.

XIII.

THE PACIFIC ISLANDS

OCEANIA, (the islands of the Southern Pacific) is divided into three parts : Polynesia — the Friendly Islands and those to the east; Micronesia — the Gilbert Islands and those to the northwest; and Melanesia — the Fijis, New Hebrides, and islands to the west of them. All three groups have an area of only 58,818 square miles — about equal to Georgia, or to England plus Wales. Their population is 875,244. The languages, though based on a common stock, are multitudinous, nearly twenty versions of the Bible being needed in the New Hebrides alone. Their primitive religions rose from mere fetichism in Melanesia to hero-worship and polytheism in Polynesia and Micronesia. Nowhere in the world have missionaries passed through experiences so tragic at the hands of cruel idolaters, and nowhere in the world have the triumphs of the gospel been more clear and complete.

TAHITI, the largest of the Society Islands, was the scene of one of the earliest and greatest of missionary triumphs. In 1796 the Duff sailed from England bearing thirty men, four being ministers and the rest tradesmen. They found two half-savage white men upon Tahiti, who served as interpreters, so that they began preaching at once.

The people were cruel in the extreme, sometimes stringing little children on a spear like beads. They worshipped hideous wooden logs.

Having made no apparent progress, the missionaries were compelled to leave in 1807. The London Missionary Society was on the point of abandoning the mission, but John Williams' pastor brought about instead a season of special prayer and letters of encouragement. The vessel bearing those letters passed on its way in October, 1813, a ship that was carrying to England the abandoned idols of the Tahitians, and the wonderful news that the gospel had triumphed in the island. It came about, under God's providence, through the prayers and labors of two native servants who had been employed in the families of the missionaries.

Soon the Gospel of Luke was translated for the islanders, who could not wait for it to be bound, so eager were they. A great missionary society was formed, and a church was built 712 feet long — so large that three pulpits were constructed, and three services held in it simultaneously.

It is sad to know that since the French took possession of the Society Islands this glorious work has suffered much hindrance and loss.

JOHN WILLIAMS, a wild youth in London, was converted as the result of a passing invitation to church given him by a good woman. He was apprentice of an iron-monger, and gained a skill in metal-working that was of the greatest value to him in later years. Hearing of the missionary triumphs in the Society Islands, he offered himself to the London Missionary Society, and was sent out in 1816, at the age of twenty, and at the same time

with Robert Moffat. At Rio de Janeiro he was so in-
dignant when he saw the system of slavery, and expressed
himself so freely, that one man tried to
stab him.

Reaching the Society Islands, he was
able to preach in the native language before the end of ten months — something
that usually required three years. Making his headquarters on the large island
of Raiatea, he taught the natives how to
build houses. To their astonishment he made chairs,
tables, sofas, and obtained a colored plaster from the coral.
He taught them how to build boats without nails. In it
all he carried out his ideal that his " words and actions
should be always pointing to the Cross."

WILLIAMS

At the end of a year it was found that the natives had
contributed $2,000 " to cause the Word of God to grow."
They built an amazing church, with turned chandeliers
made by Mr. Williams, with cocoanut shells for lamps.
The missionary encouraged the growth of the sugar cane,
and built a sugar mill. He made machinery for rope
manufacture. He drew up a code of laws, established
schools, reduced the language to writing. Hostile natives
plotted to kill him, but he continued, and baptized seventy
at his first baptism.

" I cannot content myself within a single reef," the
energetic missionary wrote; " a continent would be in-
finitely preferable." He reached out among all the sur-
rounding islands. In the Endeavor he discovered
Rarotonga, the largest of the Hervey or Cook Islands.
A heathen woman had already brought some tidings of
the gospel, and the king had named one of his children
Jehovah and another Jesus Christ. Altars to Jehovah

and Jesus Christ had been erected! The soil was ready.

Soon Williams had them praying. One chief, learning to pray from a friend, woke him up many times in the night, saying, "I have forgotten it; go over it again." At one time a long procession of natives filed past the missionary, laying their idols at his feet. In the space of seven weeks the converts built a church that would accommodate three thousand persons. They were much amazed when Mr. Williams "made a chip talk," sending thereon a written message to his wife. They would report the missionary's sermons, one listener taking the text, by previous arrangement, and the others taking one division after another. One of the strongest of the converts was a cripple without hands or feet, who used to sit by the wayside and beg bits of the Word as the more fortunate brethren returned from church.

It was on Rarotonga that our ingenious missionary constructed his famous vessel, "The Messenger of Peace," in which he explored the South Sea Islands. It was sixty feet long, and he had to build it almost without nails, fashioning his own tools. Killing the only goats in the island he made a bellows, but the rats ate the leather. Then he made an air pump for the purpose. His rudder was a piece of a pickaxe, a cooper's adz, and a long hoe. In this ship, which was only one of five that he built during his missionary life, he carried the gospel to the Samoan Islanders, and they accepted it with pathetic eagerness, becoming in great numbers "sons of the Word." The national god of war — a piece of rotten matting — was drowned. At first they thought to burn it, but decided that that would be too cruel a death!

It was while Mr. Williams was attempting to plant the

gospel in the New Hebrides, November 20, 1839, that he was murdered by the natives of Erromanga, who had just suffered severely from some of the cruel white traders, and confounded with them the loving missionary.

THE FIJI ISLANDS were entered, October 12, 1835, by William Cross and David Cargill, two Wesleyan missionaries from the Friendly Islands, and with that event began one of the most thrilling chapters in the history of the Christian church. Those islands were the central hell of earth. Cannibalism reigned there in all its most revolting cruelty. Mothers would rub pieces of human flesh over the lips of babies to give them a taste for blood. Few men lived to old age. Husbands, seized with the horrible hunger, would kill and eat their wives. Sometimes the victims were cut up alive before being placed in the ovens. Two chiefs had a record of nearly 900 whom they had eaten. Live men and women were used as rollers for the launching of the great war canoes. Men were buried alive, holding up the posts of the chiefs' houses. The sick were slain, and wives were strangled at the funeral of their husbands. Two-thirds of the children were killed at birth.

HUNT

From such a people the missionaries were exposed to fearful dangers, but fortunately many from the Friendly Islands had emigrated to Fiji, and they enjoyed the powerful aid of the Christian King George of the Friendly Islands, so that they speedily won a foothold.

In 1838 John Hunt went out from England to live there, for ten years, one of the most magnificent of mis-

sionary lives. His friend, James Calvert, accompanied
him, and labored nobly for eighteen years, winning the

"Africaner of the Fijis," King Thakombau, who chose the Christian name of
Ebenezer, while his one wife, selected
from his many wives of heathendom, became Lydia. His last act as king was to
cede Fiji to Queen Victoria in 1874,
sending her his war club.

CALVERT   Beautiful is the story of the isolated
island of Ono, whose people heard of the true God by
chance, and groped piteously after Him all alone until,
after much endeavor, they obtained a teacher; and the
story of the handsome maiden, Tovo, betrothed in infancy to a powerful king, but heroically refusing to
marry him when she became a Christian; and of the
noble Mrs. Calvert who, left alone with another missionary lady, risked her life by entering the king's house to
plead for the lives of some prisoners.

Nowhere in the world has the transforming power of
the gospel been shown so remarkably as in Fiji, where
now is a large and controlling population of lovely Christians, devout beyond the average Christian in America,
and laboring to evangelize the other less fortunate
islands.

SAMUEL MARSDEN, who was largely instrumental in
introducing Christianity among the Maoris of New Zealand, was the son of a Yorkshire blacksmith, who became
the chaplain of convicts in Australia. He was so faithful that at one time a convict, whose sins he had rebuked,
plotted to kill him by jumping into a river, pretending to
be drowning, and when Marsden tried to rescue him he

attempted to hold the preacher's head under water; but Marsden was the victor in the struggle.

Sometimes he had as many as thirty New Zealanders staying at his home, and at last he was permitted to go as a missionary among the savage people in whom he was so greatly interested. He bought the *Active* — probably the first missionary ship — and reached New Zealand in 1814, at once with superb courage going to live, unarmed, among the cannibals. He con-

MARSDEN

tinued his labors among the savages up to a great old age, winning their unbounded reverence, teaching them patiently, stopping their wars, facing a thousand perils, and becoming indeed "the Apostle of the Maoris."

GEORGE AUGUSTUS SELWYN, the first Bishop of New Zealand, organized the English Church in the Pacific. A lawyer's son, he showed great talent for legislation. From military ancestry, it was said of him that the "bishop is a general, spoiled."

When the Eton lads raced to get the good oars, Selwyn deliberately chose the one clumsy "punt pole," for he said, "I should have to pull the weight of the sulky fellow who had it; now you are all in good humor." So in after life "he took the laboring oar in everything." He was always a great oarsman, and in later years gave as his advice to young men: "*Incumbite remis,*" "Bend to your oars!"

SELWYN

"Selwyn's bush" at Eton is a famous shrub over which he would dive into the Thames. Once he walked from Cambridge to London in thirteen hours, without stopping — and in New Zealand, on his first episcopal journey around the island, 762 miles were on foot, wearing out one pair of shoes after another.

This vigorous young man became a curate, with special interest in a charity kitchen he established, and in 1841 he was made the first bishop of New Zealand. A clerk's error added 68° to his diocese, extending it to 34° N instead of 34° S — a mistake that made possible Selwyn's splendid work in Melanesia.

During the six months' voyage out, the young bishop learned navigation so thoroughly that a ship's captain once said it almost made him a Christian to see the bishop bring his schooner into harbor. He also learned Maori so that he could preach in the native language the first Sunday after his arrival. He landed in May, 1842, his first act being to kneel in prayer upon the beach.

For twenty-six years Selwyn labored in the South Seas. His cathedral was " a mean wooden structure painted white." He early established a training college for native preachers.

Over the Maoris, just emerged from horrible cannibalism, he won a powerful ascendency. He took long and arduous journeys among the islands, bringing back natives for instruction. With his own hands out of an old sail he made a garment for the first female scholar he took on board his ship. During a visit home Selwyn's addresses were so inspiring that one young man, possessed of $60,000, offered all of it to the mission — an offer which, however, was refused.

During the sad nine years' war with the natives, Selwyn was in many a battle, ministering to the wounded on both sides, and always to the Maori first. As a result of that war the natives largely fell away from their Christianity, and even the good bishop himself became an object of their undiscriminating hatred. When, in 1868, Selwyn reluctantly became Bishop of Lichfield, in England, he left seven bishops in the South Seas where he had taken up the work unaided.

JOHN COLERIDGE PATTESON was the son of an honored English judge, and a descendant of Coleridge, the poet. He was naturally devout, a Bible-reader from infancy. They called him once in the nursery, and he begged for a few minutes, just to "finish the binding of Satan for a thousand years."

He had grit, and once he bore in silence for three weeks a broken collar bone because he "did not like to make

PATTESON

a fuss." He resigned his cricket captaincy at Eton because certain boys at the annual dinner insisted on singing objectionable songs, and would not return till promises of amendment were made.

"Lady Patteson, will you give me Coley?" asked the good Bishop Selwyn, and in 1855 he actually accompanied the bishop to his New Zealand diocese. On the way he learned Maori so thoroughly (having always a wonderful gift for languages) that on his first Sunday after arriving he preached to the natives with great success.

For five years he shared Selwyn's labors of teaching and visiting the islands, often in great perils from the deep and the natives, and when dreaming of home saying to himself, "Look around the horizon, and see how many islands you can count!" In 1861 he was made first bishop of the Melanesian islands, and prosecuted his work there with characteristic ardor. At one time, surrounded by would-be murderers, he fell on his knees and began to pray for them. They did not understand a word, but were so struck with his demeanor that they conducted him courteously to his ship.

The iniquitous white traders, who kidnapped the natives in their "kill-kill" vessels and "snatch-snatch" ships, would decoy the blacks on board by pretending that their beloved bishop was there, themselves carrying Bibles in their hands. At Nukapu of the Santa Cruz group, they had painted their ship in imitation of Patteson's, and through this artifice stolen into slavery some of the natives. Soon afterward Patteson visited the island on his errand of love, and the ignorant, heartbroken savages killed him in revenge, pushing his body out to his friends marked with five wounds, one for each of the kidnapped natives. When the islanders learned whom they had slain, they drove the murderers from the island, and shot the native who had given the first blow.

JOHN G. PATON, "The King of the Cannibals," as Spurgeon called him, has a story probably the most thrilling of all in missionary annals. He was born in 1824, the son of a pious Scotch stocking-maker and colporteur. After successful work as city missionary in Glasgow, in 1858 he was sent to the New Hebrides by the Reformed Presbyterian Church.

Landed on the small island of Tanna, he spent four years among the most bloodthirsty men on earth. In 1848 John Geddie of Nova Scotia, and in 1852 John Inglis of Scotland had gone to the island of Aneityum, and in a few years had won them marvellously to the gospel. The natives saved for fifteen years until they had the $6,000 required for a Bible in their own language.

It was a native teacher from Aneityum, faithful old Abraham, who stood by Mr. Paton through all the desperate scenes on Tanna.

After three months the missionary's young wife had died, and Patteson and Selwyn — calling in their mission ship — wept with him over her grave. The treacherous natives compelled him to pay three times for the site of his house. They stole everything he had, and only the chance visit of an English ship of war induced them, with comical haste, to bring back their plunder.

PATON

Paton made a bold stand against wife-beating, widow-strangling, the eating of human flesh. Iniquitous traders, with the fiendish purpose of killing off the natives, kidnapped one of them, exposed him to measles, and sent him back to introduce the plague, which swept away a third of the island's population. Thirteen of Paton's party died, and the rest sailed away in despair, leaving him alone with old Abraham.

Maddened Tannese, confounding together all white men, determined upon Paton's destruction. In 1861 came the news of the martyrdom of the Nova Scotian missionaries, G. N. Gordon and his wife, on Erromanga, and Paton seemed destined also to perish.

Time after time he grasped the war clubs raised against him, avoided the killing-stone, or struck up the levelled musket. A dying native thrust a murderous knife at him. Sometimes his faithful dog Clutha saved him; sometimes a useless little revolver; sometimes friendly natives; more often the mysterious, direct providence of God, as when, for instance, a raging band of savages surrounded his premises and set fire to them, and were

MISSIONARY PIONEERS.	MISSIONS IN THE ISLANDS.
(*Carey in India.*) 1793—	—1796. The Duff sails.
(*Morrison in China.*) 1807—	—1809. Obookiah.
(*Judson in Burma.*) 1813—	—1814. Marsden.
	—1816. Williams.
(*Fisk in Syria.*) 1819—	—1819. Bingham. Thurston.
(*Gutzlaff in Siam.*) 1828—	
(*Goodell in Turkey.*) 1831—	
(*Perkins in Persia.*) 1833—	—1833. Lyman. Munson.
	—1834. Coan.
	—1835. Cross. Cargill.
	—1838. Hunt. Calvert.
	—1839. Williams killed.
	—1842. Selwyn.
	—1848. Geddie.
	—1852. Inglis. Gulick. Sturges. Snow.
	—1855. Patteson.
(*Williams in Japan.*) 1859—	—1858. Paton.
	—1861. Gordons killed.
	—1863. Hawaii mission closed
	—1866. Chalmers.
	—1871. Macfarlane. Patteson killed.
	—1874. Fiji ceded to England. Logan.
(*Allen in Korea.*) 1884—	—1887. Spain in Carolines.
	—1900. Germany in Carolines.
	—1901. Chalmers killed.

dispersed (the fire being at the same time quenched) by the sudden downpour of a tropical storm.

Amid a thousand perils the missionary at last escaped from Tanna, only to pass to the nearby island of Aniwa, which has been transformed by his labors into a Christian community whose godliness is an example to many more favored lands. It was the sinking of a well — the unheard-of rain from below — that broke the back of heathenism on Aniwa. The native gods never helped them in that way!

Here also, however, many perils were encountered, as once when the mission house was surrounded by savages who had resolved to murder the missionaries, and Paton's little boy in some way got out of the house, and to his father's horror went right among the armed men, scolded them : " Naughty ! Naughty ! " and by his prattle won them to peace. Often they toiled in deep anguish, as when Paton and his wife were unable, through sickness, to move, and their baby died and was buried while they were in that sad plight, their other little children singing a hymn by the grave. But they had much to cheer them, as when the orphan children whom Paton tended, getting food after a time of famine, stood waiting with their eyes fixed eagerly upon it. " What are you waiting for ? " asked Paton. " For you to thank God for it, and ask His blessing on it."

Now, through the labors of the missionary Watts, even Tanna has been won to Christ, and, largely through Paton's words and writings, heroic missionaries have changed the character of all the southern portion of the New Hebrides.

AMERICAN MISSIONS in Oceania are carried on by the Congregationalists ; the Seventh-Day Adventists (Society Islands) ; the Episcopalians, who have begun work in Hawaii ; the Disciples of Christ (Hawaii and the Philippines), Methodists North (the Philippines), and the Presbyterians, Baptists, and United Brethren in the Philippines. The work in the Philippines, and present-day work in Hawaii, must be reserved for a home-mission study.

HENRY OBOOKIAH, a dark-skinned boy, was found in 1809 weeping on the doorsteps of Yale College. He had drifted from the Sandwich Islands. He was longing for an education, and that the true religion should be carried to his native land. His pathetic story led to the missionary effort for Hawaii, which began on October 23, 1819, when Hiram Bingham, Asa Thurston, three native Hawaiians, and Americans of various trades, a party of seventeen, set sail from Boston for the Sandwich Islands.

They were met, on landing, by the surprising story that a revolution had just overthrown the old heathen gods, and the land was without a religion. Then began one of the most wonderful triumphs of gospel history. The rulers became Christian. The Princess Kapiolani defied the crater goddess, Pele, hurling stones into the sacred lava, and worshipping the true God in the presence of the awe-struck idolaters. The horrible diseases which were destroying the people were checked by forbidding the evil intercourse with foreign sailors — a step which often brought the missionaries in peril of their lives from the hands of angry Englishmen and Americans.

TITUS COAN witnessed the climax of Hawaiian missions. He was a Connecticut farmer's boy who, after an experience in school-teaching, decided in his early manhood for the missionary calling. His first undertaking was a hazardous expedition, under the American Board, to Patagonia in 1834. He was captured by the savages, but fortunately escaped. In December of the same year he set sail for the Sandwich Islands, and reached Honolulu after a voyage of six months around Cape Horn. From there he travelled about two hundred miles to his station, Hilo, on the largest island, Hawaii. The stupid captain lost his reckoning, returned to Honolulu and had to start over again.

COAN

At the end of three months the young missionary preached his first sermon in the native language. Be-

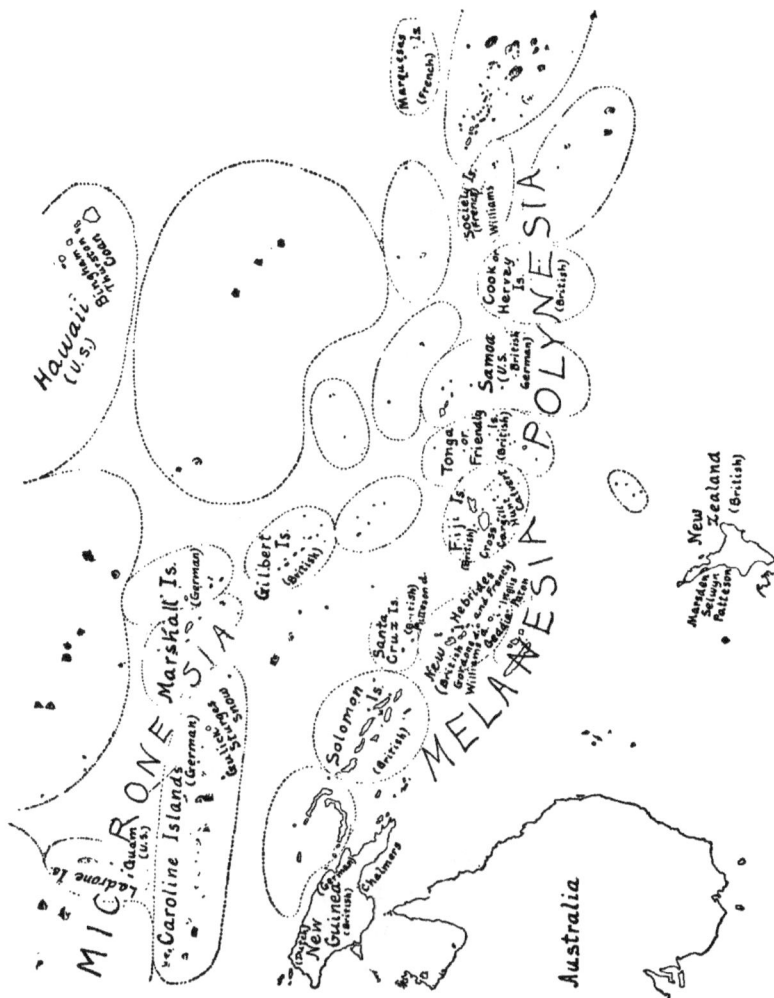

Marquesas Is. (French)

Society Is. (French)
Williams

Cook or Hervey Is. (British)

Samoa (U.S. British German)

Hawaii (U.S.)

Tonga or Friendly Is. (British)

Cross

Fiji Is. (British)

New Zealand (British)

Gilbert Is. (British)

Marshall Is. (German)

Gulick and Snow

Santa Cruz Is. (British)

New Hebrides (British & French) Gordon and Williams

Marsden Selwyn Patteson

MICRONESIA

POLYNESIA

MELANESIA

Caroline Islands (German)

Guam (U.S.)

Ladrone Is.

Solomon Is. (British)

New Guinea (British) Chalmers

Australia

fore the close of the year he had made on foot and by canoe the circuit of the island — three hundred miles. The world's greatest volcano has torn the island into many ravines most difficult to cross. There were no roads, nor horses, nor bridges. Mr. Coan crossed the tumultuous streams often at peril of his life. Sometimes the natives formed a chain of strong men across a river, and he made his way from one friendly support to the next. Sometimes a rope was thrown across, lassoing boughs on the opposite shore, and served as a stay in the dangerous transit. His ocean canoe trips around the island often brought him in perils of the deep.

The fruit of his faithful and unwearied labors began to come in large abundance in 1836. Great numbers flocked around him. They would keep him till midnight preaching to them, and crowd the house again at cockcrowing. The villages begged for him. " I preached in three of them before breakfast," he records. "When the meeting closed at one village, most of the people ran on to the next."

Hilo was the centre of interest. Its population grew from 1,000 to 10,000. The old and the feeble were carried thither for fifty miles in litters. There was a two-year Pentecost. They built a meeting-house for 2,000 souls, and arranged that while one division of the people filled it for the sermon, the others should meet elsewhere and pray. Loud outcries, tremblings, swoonings, weeping, irresistibly burst in upon the preacher. Mockers were struck dumb and fell senseless. A vast tidal wave that swept away many houses and destroyed many lives deepened the impression. The more violent demonstrations were not encouraged by the missionaries, but could not be repressed.

The utmost care was taken to prove the people's sincerity before baptizing any of them. Nevertheless, before 1870, Mr. Coan had himself baptized and received into the church 11,960 persons. On the first Sabbath of July, 1838, occurred one of the happiest events since Pentecost — the baptism at one time by Mr. Coan of 1,705 tested converts.

A great church was built, costing $13,000, the natives making a dedication offering of $1,239 that the structure might be dedicated free from debt.

All the remainder of Mr. Coan's life was given to Hawaii. In 1882, when he was nearly eighty-two years old, he was stricken with paralysis during a revival into which he was throwing all his splendid enthusiasm, and thus passed away upon the battle-field.

A MISSION CLOSED. — In 1863 Hawaii was recognized as a Christian nation, and the American Board handed over the work to the Hawaiian Evangelical Association, which, however, is largely maintained by the white people. The native Hawaiians have been splendid factors in the evangelization of the Marquesas, Marshall, and Gilbert Islands. The work in the first named was the result of the visit of a Marquesan chief who went to Hawaii to beg that Christian teachers should be sent to his people also, and the Hawaiians gladly responded. The missionary work in Hawaii now carried on by the Hawaiian Association is among the natives and the imported foreign laborers — Chinese, Japanese, and Portuguese.

MICRONESIA was occupied by the American Board in 1852, sending L. H. Gulick, A. A. Sturges, and B. G. Snow, and two Hawaiians, all with their wives. They settled upon the islands of Kusaie and Ponape in the Carolines, and from there the work has spread to Ruk and other islands of the group, as well as throughout the neighboring Gilbert and Marshall Islands.

A great aid in this work has been the four Morning Stars and other vessels, many of them wrecked in those treacherous seas. The mission ship cruises among the islands, and gathers the natives to central schools in the various languages at Kusaie. All the missionary workers upon the Gilbert Islands are Hawaiians.

ROBERT WILLIAM LOGAN was an Ohio boy who, after a service in the Civil War that cost him his health for life, went through a medical school, and in 1874 became a missionary of the American Board to the Carolines. The new converts on Ponape, eager themselves to undertake mission work, had sent three men and their wives to introduce Christianity into the Mortlock Islands to the west. They had succeeded marvellously, and five thousand had become Christians. Mr. Logan set himself to further this work with instruction and translation.

LOGAN

On a hot, lonely island he was seized with a hemorrhage of the lungs. The Morning Star was delayed. After long waiting, his noble wife placed him upon a little trading vessel, beneath an awning on the deck, and sat by the side of her uncomplaining husband all the long way to New Zealand.

He lived, and returned to the island of Ruk, where Moses, a magnificent native, had begun a remarkable work, in the development of which Logan spent his strength till in 1887 he passed away, saying on his deathbed, "It is God's work, and it is worth all it costs." For

several years his heroic wife all alone kept up the work
in that difficult and isolated field.

In 1887 the Spaniards took possession of the Caroline
Islands, sending a governor and six priests to Ponape.
The missionary in charge was arrested on absurd charges
and sent to Manila, but the governor there released him.
In his absence the natives revolted from Spanish oppres-
sion, and the missionaries, who tried to maintain peace,
were banished, the mission property being destroyed.

At the close of our war with Spain the Carolines were
sold to Germany, who governs the neighboring Marshall
Islands, and in 1900 the American missionaries returned
to Ponape, being received cordially as the guests of the
German governor. During the long interim, left entirely
to themselves and under the urgent pressure of Catholicism, the native Christians had maintained their faith and
their worship. The Germans have required the use of the
German instead of the English language, but they agreed
not to interfere with the missions. The disquieting news,
however, has just reached this country to the effect that
on pretence of seditious conduct the members of the
graduating class of the training-school at Ruk have been
seized and imprisoned.

AUSTRALIA still contains about 28,000 aborigines,
chiefly in Queensland. They are among the lowest of
human races, and are rapidly disappearing, but ten missionary societies are at work to bring them to the Saviour,
none of these being American.

NEW GUINEA is the world's largest island, with an
area of 312,329 square miles, the Dutch owning the western half, the Germans the northeastern quarter, and the
English the southeastern quarter. There are 660,000

natives, whose religion is very rudimentary, being a compound of spirit-worship and ancestor-worship. Though Dutch and German societies are at work, by far the most important missionary labors are those connected with the British portion, which were established in 1871 by Dr. Macfarlane. The most distinguished missionaries have been Dr. W. G. Lawes, organizer of a notable missionary training-school, and Rev. James Chalmers.

JAMES CHALMERS, the London Missionary Society's pioneer missionary to New Guinea, was a Scotch Highlander, born in 1841 — the son of a stone mason. The hardy lad was three times almost drowned, and when ten years old he made a wonderful rescue of another by his swimming.

He was about fifteen when he heard of the gospel work among the Fijis, and, kneeling in a lonely place beside a wall, prayed God to make him a missionary. After work in the Glasgow slums and theological training — in the course of which he saved another life from drowning — on January 4, 1866, he sailed in the second John Williams for the South Seas.

He reached Rarotonga, in the Cook Islands, after a voyage of seven months, after great hazards, the total wreck of the missionary ship, and rescue in a pirate vessel, over whose desperate captain Chalmers won great influence. For ten years "Tamate," as the natives called him — that being as near as they could get to "Chalmers" — lived at Rarotonga, teaching school, fighting strong drink, and training up a large company of heroic native Christians, who became his beloved and trusted assistants in New Guinea, dying there, many of them, for their Saviour.

But the missionary's vigorous spirit chafed in the quite civilized Cook Islands, and in 1877 Chalmers entered upon his splendid life work, settling among absolute savages at Suau on the southeast coast of New Guinea. He was alone among cannibals, who brought his wife, as a delicate attention, a man's breast, cooked. They were back in the Stone Age. They were cruel, treacherous, fiercely covetous of the missionary's goods, his only means of barter and of food supply. Death was threatened if these were refused, but Chalmers' heroic wife, the question being left with her, voted to stay and face the death.

CHALMERS

Their lives were saved through a thousand perils. Always unarmed, "Tamate" went boldly among the wild tribes, and his powerful body and masterful spirit gained over them the influence of authority. He wrenched from the murderous hand the club raised to slay him. He ate freely with bands of poisoners. When an assassin crept up behind, he turned and calmly ordered him in front of him. Once an attacking party was halted at the fence of his house by an unseen irresistible force. At death's door with fever, he summoned his will, bade his natives stick his pipe in his mouth, and grimly refused to die.

He became the "Great Heart of New Guinea," as his friend Robert Louis Stevenson called him. His dauntless explorations made him the Livingstone of New Guinea. His leadership of the natives made it easy for Great Britain to extend a protectorate over southeastern New Guinea, and in 1888 to annex it.

Pressing eagerly westward along the coast of the great

island, "Tamate" brought tribe after tribe to a knowledge of Jesus Christ. At one time 450 converted savages gathered around him for a communion service, a famous robber chief acting as the leading deacon. On the evening of Easter Sunday, April 7, 1901, the intrepid missionary was murdered by a tribe he was newly approaching on his errand of peace and love. His native helper, soon after his death, petitioned to be sent as missionary to the village that had slain his beloved leader.

THE MALAY ARCHIPELAGO, including Dutch New Guinea, has an area of nearly one million square miles — one-third that of the United States. The Dutch own most of the region, and the greater part of the missionary work is therefore done by the Dutch and German societies. Mohammedanism has great power in these islands, and more converts have been won from the Moslems here than anywhere else in the world. Nearly 20,000 Mohammedans have been converted in Java. The most famous American missionaries to this region are Lyman and Munson.

HENRY LYMAN, a Massachusetts boy, was the leader of the wild set at Amherst, but was converted in a college revival, and with his friend, Samuel Munson, he was sent by the American Board in 1833 to the East Indies. On the fly-leaf of all his journals this ardent young man was in the habit of writing:

600,000,000

ARE PERISHING!!

Calvary.

"Suppose the Board does not send you on a mission?" a friend once suggested. "Then," he replied, "I will work my passage on some ship; for, the Lord willing, I am determined to go."

Animated by this spirit, after study of Malay and Chinese and instruction from Medhurst in Java, the two missionaries set out on a preliminary exploration of the islands, and ventured even into the interior of Sumatra among the Battas, scaling dangerous precipices and piercing dense jungles. There, in the summer of 1834, they were set upon by two hundred armed natives at Sacca. They themselves had arms, which they used against wild beasts, but gave them up to the mob. Notwithstanding this, Munson was run through with a spear, and Lyman was shot, the first being thirty and the second only twenty-four years old. When the natives learned what good men had been murdered, they burned Sacca and killed many of the villagers.

PN
Erwin
Bryant Pond
PN
Caracas
CA
VENEZUELA
Austin
Güttner
Schumann
Dähne
Hartman
GUIANA
Br. Du. Fr.
Pratt PN
Bogota
COLOMBIA
ABS
ECUADOR
MN CA
Manaos
SB
Para
SB
PERU
Callao Lima MN
Penzotta
ABS
Cuzco
Jarrett
Peters
SDA
CB
La Paz
OA
BOLIVIA
ABS Sucre
Mongiardino
PARAGUAY MN
Wood
Grubb
BRAZIL
ABS
YMCA
SF
SDA
CA
PS
PS
PS
PS
Pernambuco
PS SB
Bahia
PN. SB
PN
MS
SB
PS MS PN
SB Spaulding
Rio de Janeiro Simonton
PN PS
Sao Paulo
PN
Villegagn
Boles
Chambarlin
Bagby
PN
ARGENTINE
REPUBLIC
ABS MN
Buenos Ayres
Goodfellow
SDA
CA SA
SF
MS
E
URUGUAY
Thomson
MN
OA
PN
Trumbull
Santiago
Taylor
MN
CHILI
PATAGONIA
Gardiner
Tierra del Fuego

American Missions in
South America.

ABS—American Bible Society.
CA—Christian and Missionary Alliance.
CB—Canadian Baptists.
E—Episcopalian.
MN—Methodists, North.
MS—Methodists, South.
PN—Presbyterians, North.
PS—Presbyterians, South.
SA—Salvation Army.
SB—Southern Baptists.
SDA—Seventh-Day Adventists.
SF—Seaman's Friend Society.

XIV.

SOUTH AMERICA

"THE NEGLECTED CONTINENT" is a name rightly applied to South America. Vast regions yet remain unoccupied by missionaries and untouched by true religion. And yet the United States, by proclaiming the Monroe Doctrine, and insisting upon it with much force, has made herself peculiarly responsible for the nations to the south. Instead of doing less for South America than for other continents, we should be doing more.

WHY MISSIONS IN SOUTH AMERICA at all? Does not Roman Catholicism hold sway there, and is not that a form of Christianity? Yes, but even Catholics from the United States repudiate the degraded Catholicism of South America, and recognize it as a form of heathenism. Here as nowhere else in the world Catholicism shows what it can do when given three centuries of undisputed control. The priests are abominably licentious. Among the people the social evil is rampant. Gambling flourishes, with lotteries sometimes even patronized by the church. Intemperance is universal. Ignorance is everywhere. The governments are fiercely bigoted. Superstitions of the lowest sort hold the people in serfdom. Under the mask of religion, secret infidelity abounds. Under the pretence of political freedom there is political tyranny often, and always political instability. The constitutions of all these republics are modelled upon our own ; but they have the form without the substance, which is our Protestant faith and character.

THE PROBLEM is that of a continent of seven million square miles, one-seventh of the land surface of the world, nobly variegated with superb mountain ranges, marvellous plains, a grand river system reaching everywhere, and a wealth in the products of mine, forest, and field, still practically undeveloped yet not excelled by any region of the globe. The nations are learning this, and immigration is rapidly growing, especially from Europe. Every year greatly increases the number to be won in South America. It is a most strategic point.

This great continent is occupied by about thirty-eight million persons, perhaps half the population of the United States. Most of these are Spanish-speaking (and, in Brazil, Portuguese-speaking) descendants of the Catholic conquerors. About five million, however, are Indians.

THE INDIANS are found everywhere, especially in Patagonia and the interior forests of Brazil, where one may easily travel three thousand miles without meeting a missionary. The descendants of the proud race of Incas, in adopting Catholicism they merely changed their idols. They are a sturdy race, however, with great possibilities and not difficult to reach. One chief travelled a thousand miles to Sao Paulo in Brazil to beg for some Christian teacher for his people. Allen Gardiner was the pioneer missionary to the South American Indians.

ALLEN GARDINER led perhaps the most strenuous and original of all missionary lives. As a boy he preferred to sleep on the floor in order to train himself to hardships. He was an Englishman, and distinguished himself as a "middy" in the English navy, becoming a lieutenant.

His heart was won to God through the touching record of his mother's last days written by his father, and given him by a friend. Watching a bookstore till it was empty of witnesses he crept in and bought a Bible. After seeing the results

GARDINER

of missionary work on Tahiti, he became a missionary enthusiast, and a visit in his ship to South America inspired him with an undying desire to benefit the neglected Indians of that continent. Beside the coffin of his beloved wife he solemnly dedicated himself to God's service.

First he went to South Africa, where amid a thousand perils he aided the establishment of the town of Durban, and gained such influence over the ferocious Zulu chief, Dingaan, that the Zulu made him governor of the region now known as Natal. Difficulties between the whites and the Zulus broke up his missionary labors, and with a sad heart he turned to South America in 1838.

From that year till his death in 1851, his time was spent alternately in the most extensive missionary travel, visiting repeatedly all parts of the continent, and in frequent returns to England, pleading for the means to establish his mission, he himself lavishing his all upon it. His journeys through the wilds of South America, his encounters with the bigoted Catholics and the crafty and ungrateful Indians, his labors in the distribution of Bibles, his narrow escapes, his ceaseless energy, make a most romantic and inspiriting story.

Finally, with a surgeon, a catechist, three Cornish
fishermen, and a ship carpenter who declared that to be
under Captain Gardiner "was like a heaven on earth,
he was such a man of prayer," he entered upon the
saddest of all missionary enterprises, an attempt to gain
a missionary foothold among the savages on the bleak
coast of Tierra del Fuego. The expedition was very
inadequately fitted out. By a terrible error they had
left on shipboard their powder and shot, and could not
shoot game, almost the only resource on those desolate
shores. One relief boat was wrecked, and the captain of
the other disobeyed orders and did not visit them. The
ice tore their nets so that they could not catch fish.

During nine months they managed to prolong a
wretched existence, and at last one by one they starved
to death, the heroic Gardiner himself probably the last to
fall. The two captains that came at last cried like
children upon finding their dead bodies. Upon a rock
they had painted Ps. 62 : 5–8 : "My soul, wait thou only
upon God : for my expectation is from him." Gardiner's
journal, preserved as by a miracle, and his martyr's
death, accomplished what his life could not bring about,
and soon the missionary schooner, *Allen Gardiner*, sailed
from England to establish on firm foundations the Fue-
gian Mission, which is only one of the enterprises of the
South American Missionary Society.

DUTCH GUIANA, or Surinam, was the earliest South
American mission field, and starting there, we will trav-
erse the continent southward and then northward along
the west coast. Dutch Guiana is a triumph of Protestantism and of the Moravians. Here are the almost savage bush negroes, descendants of run-away slaves from

the West Indies, full of immorality and the most gross superstition. John Güttner and Christopher Dähne, landing in 1738, were the first missionaries. Then came in 1748 Theophilus Solomon Schumann, a gifted professor, "The Apostle of the Arawak Indians."

Louis Dähne, laboring in solitude among the Indians, was lying stricken with fever when a huge snake bit him and coiled violently around him. Fearing that the Indians would be charged with his death, the heroic man grasped a piece of chalk and wrote quickly, "A snake has killed me." But at once Christ's promise concerning serpents (Mark 16 : 18) came to his mind, he flung the snake away, and took no harm.

The first missionaries among the negroes supported themselves by carrying on a bakery and a tailor shop, and ever since the Moravian missionaries have been self-supporting. Among the noblest of the missionaries to the blacks was Mary Hartmann, who, in 1848, went alone into the wilderness, and until her death in 1853 patiently organized Christian peace, purity, and industry among the wild people. Only once during that time did she permit herself to return to civilization, and that for but a single day.

Surinam is called "Dead Man's Land." Nowhere on earth, perhaps, is there a more difficult climate. For the first fifty years of the mission there were more missionary deaths than converts. Now, however, as the fruit of these glorious labors, practically the whole population is Christian, and Dutch Guiana is no longer a mission field.

BRITISH GUIANA, or Demerara, is worked by English societies, and especially by the great Society for the Propagation of the Gospel, the first bishop (1842) being William Piercy Austin, who labored with great success for half a century.   Four thousand Chinese have entered the country, all of whom have been converted.   They are well-to-do and support their own churches, making fine missionary assistants when they return to China.   About forty per cent. of the people are imported Hindu laborers, and only about two per cent. of these have yet been won for Christ.

In French Guiana no Protestant missionary society is at work.

BRAZIL was for three centuries the largest possession of Portugal.   In 1822 Dom Pedro I. became emperor, and in 1831 Dom Pedro II., who, though an admirable monarch, was quietly deposed, largely through the efforts of the philosopher and statesman, Benjamin Constant, "The Founder of the Republic."   "The United States of Brazil," thus formed, was closely modelled upon our own country, with church absolutely separate from state, with civil marriage and religious freedom.

Brazil is nearly as large as the United States and half as large as all South America, but its population is only fifteen million, chiefly along the coast, where, therefore, the missions chiefly lie.   It is a splendid, rich, though undeveloped empire, whose greatest feature is the un-equalled Amazon, navigable by ocean steamers to the boundaries of Peru.

Half of this immense territory inland is occupied by about 800,000 Indians, for whom very little missionary work is carried on.   Along the coast, however, ten American societies are at work — the Bible Society, with a most effective and blessed system of colportage ; the Adventists; the Christian Alliance; the Y. M. C. A., which does its best work for South America in Brazil; the Episcopalians, who began their work in 1889 with the American Church Missionary Society; the Seamen's Friend Society; the Presbyterians South and North, and the Southern Methodists and Baptists.

Brazil came near being Protestant. In 1555 a French knight, Nicholas Durand de Villegagnon, led a colony of persecuted Huguenots sent out by the good Admiral Coligny, and settled them on a small island now overlooked by Rio de Janeiro. Calvin was interested in the project, and sent them ministers. Villegagnon, however, "The Cain of America" as he was called, proved treacherous, slew three of the leaders, drove many of them to the Catholic mainland, and forced the rest to return to Europe in a leaky boat where five or six died of starvation on the long voyage. The learned and eloquent John Boles, the last of the French Huguenots, lingered in misery for eight years in a Jesuit prison, and was then put to death on the site of Rio de Janeiro — the first South American martyr.

The Dutch made a slight attempt at missionary work in 1640, but, on the whole, Brazil was left in darkest religious destitution. Henry Martyn, on his way to India in 1805, mourned over the scene. "When shall this beautiful country," he cried, "be delivered from idolatry and spurious Christianity? Crosses there are in abundance, but when shall the doctrine of the Cross be held up?"

The first to answer Martyn's cry were the Northern Methodists, whose pioneer missionary was Justin Spaulding, who went to Rio in 1836. This work, however, was abandoned in 1841.

The next to go from America were the Presbyterians, whose pioneer in 1859 was A. G. Simonton. His first audience came out of courtesy to him — two men whom he had been teaching English. His first church — formed in 1862 — consisted of two members.

The Southern Presbyterians soon followed — in 1869 — and have happily united now with the Northern Presbyterians in the one Synod of Brazil, with seven flourishing presbyteries, containing many self-supporting churches. Scarcely one in seven of the Brazilians can read and write, so that education is an important missionary tool. The leading Protestant institution in South America is Mackenzie College at Sao Paulo, finely developed through his forty years of service by the Presbyterian missionary, Dr. George W. Chamberlain. Among its more than 500 students there are four Catholics to every Protestant.

The Southern Baptist Mission in Brazil is, like the large work of the Southern Methodists, the only mission of their denomination in South America. The Baptist first to make a permanent beginning was W. B. Bagby, whose zealous labors aroused Catholic hostility. He was knocked down while preaching, and he and his wife were arrested as he was about to baptize some converts. His preaching-place was stoned by a mob, church-members were driven from their homes and business. In one locality baptisms had to be held in a river at night at some distance from the city. Here, however, as everywhere else, persecution has simply driven deeper the foundations of the faith.

PARAGUAY was occupied in 1886 by the arrival of Thomas B. Wood, LL. D., of the Methodist church, which still conducts the only American work in that country. One important result of Dr. Wood's labors was the recognition of the civil rights of Protestants, especially giving legal sanction to their marriages, for before his arrival the Catholic church had a monopoly of that sacred ceremony. This was accomplished only after months of arduous and courageous toil.

Among the Chaco Indians of Paraguay a notable work is being done by the South American Missionary Society, who, coming in 1888, found the way prepared for them by an ancient Indian tradition that some day men, not Indians but looking like them, should come and teach them about the spirit land. Their leader, the gallant W. B. Grubb, had at one time a narrow escape from death, but no missionary life has been lost, though the Indians were so dangerous that the Paraguay government wished to provide the first missionary band with a military escort.

URUGUAY, the smallest of the South American republics, is continued in existence in order that neither of those jealous neighbors, Brazil and the Argentine Republic, may control the great Plata River. There are few Indians here, and the population is largely made up of recent arrivals from southern Europe. A strong colony of Waldensians, here as in their native Italy, hold forth the true religion. The chief missionary factor is the Methodist Church North, whose work was established in 1868 by Dr. J. F. Thomson in the handsome city of Montevideo.

THE ARGENTINE REPUBLIC rivals Brazil in its commercial possibilities, and excels it in the matter of its temperate climate. It was the first of the South American countries to win freedom from Spain, and its army aided in gaining independence for Chile and Peru. Buenos Ayres, with its more than three-quarters of a million inhabitants, is a great cosmopolitan city, with many thousands of careless, money-making Protestants to care for as well as the Catholics.

The immigration hither exceeds, in proportion to the population, that to the United States. Baron Hirsch founded in the republic a large colony of Jews as a refuge for this oppressed people. Our missions here have never met with violence or persecution.

They were begun by the Methodists of the North in 1836, their work being still the leading one, with its important press at Buenos Ayres, and its educational centre at Rosario. Rev. William Goodfellow was a notable missionary, and here also has labored for nearly half a century Dr. John F. Thomson, whose powerful controversies with representatives of the Church of Rome have drawn wide notice to Protestantism. On one occasion, after such a public dispute with Father Mansueto, putting the question to vote he carried the day unanimously, and about two hundred followed the *padre* fourteen blocks to his own door, loudly expressing their contempt for him.

The Seventh Day Adventists, the Christian Alliance, the Seaman's Friend Society, the American Bible Society, and the Salvation Army also labor in the Argentine Republic.

CHILE, with an average breadth of only about 200 miles, has the enormous length of 2,700 miles, and would stretch clear across the United States. Its northern 800 miles is a rainless desert. Its enormous deposits of nitrate of soda are famous; it has also great mineral and agricultural wealth. Santiago, its capital, surrounded by an amphitheatre of glorious mountains, is a beautiful city, which was nearly eighty years old when the Pilgrim Fathers landed at Plymouth. Government here has been more stable than in the other South American republics.

The principal missionary work is done by the Presbyterians, established in 1873, and the Methodists North, established in 1878. William Taylor began the Methodist work, placing it upon his well-known platform of self-support. It has ever since retained that character, and is one of the most prosperous missions on the continent.

—1555. Boles.
—1732. Dober. Nitschman.
—1738. Guttner. Dahne.
—1786. Coke.

(*Carey in India.*) 1793—
(*The Duff sails.*) 1796—
(*Morrison in China.*) 1807— —1805. Martyn in Brazil.
(*Judson in Burma.*) 1813—
(*Fisk in Syria.*) 1819—
(*Gutzlaff in Siam.*) 1828—
(*Goodell in Turkey.*) 1831— —1831. *Dom Pedro II.*
(*Perkins in Persia.*) 1833—
—1836. Spaulding.
—1838. Gardiner.
—1842. Austin.
—1845. Trumbull.
—1848. Hartmann. Moravians in Nicaragua.
—1851. Gardiner dies.
—1856. Pratt.
—1857. *Mexico grants religious liberty.*
(*Williams in Japan.*) 1859— —1859. Simonton.
—1866. Rankin.
—1868. Thomson.
—1869. Riley.
—1872. Stephens.
—1873. Butler.
—1878. Taylor.
—1880. Westrup killed.
—1882. Hill.
(*Allen in Korea.*) 1884— —1884. Bryant. *Diaz president of Mexico.*
—1886. Wood.
—1888. Grubb.
—1889. *Brazil a republic.*
—1895. Jarrett. Peters.
—1896. *Ecuador grants religious liberty.*
—1897. Pond.

MISSIONS IN
SOUTH AND CENTRAL AMERICA,
MEXICO, AND THE
WEST INDIES.

The first missionary to Chile was Dr. David Trumbull, who reached Valparaiso when he was twenty-six years old, on Christmas Day, 1845, at a time when there was not a single missionary upon the continent. He gave a long and most manly life to the work, dying in 1889.

BOLIVIA, more than two and a half miles above the sea level, is the loftiest of countries, and its superb Lake Titicaca is the highest body of water on earth. An island in this lake was the central abode of the old empire of the Incas — the "Heroic Age" of South America.

This vast region, though rich in minerals beyond other portions of the continent, has but few railroads, and is less developed even than other parts of South America. More than half of the people are Indians, degenerate descendants of the proud Incas, superstitious Catholics, and some of the tribes so ignorant that they can count only to five, and in the case of one tribe only as far as one.

The American Bible Society has done magnificent pioneer work during these years when bitter persecution has prevented settled missions, and its colporteurs have labored with undaunted heroism. One of them, JOSÉ MONGIARDINO, even penetrated as far as Sucre, sold his books, and was on the way back to Argentina for more when the Catholics set upon him in a lonely place, murdered him, and buried him between the graves of a murderer and a suicide. Later, the veteran agent of the Bible Society, ANDREW M. MILNE, "The Livingstone of South America," dared to visit his grave with Penzotti, and there the two consecrated their lives anew to the redemption of South America.

Now the beginnings of permanent work have been

made by the Baptists of Canada at La Paz, the capital, and at Oruro. The Seventh Day Adventists also labor there.

PERU AND ECUADOR constitute the rest of the old Incas' realm, and their story is precisely like that of Bolivia. Mission work in all three countries did not begin till after 1888. Ecuador, the last of the South American republics to establish religious liberty, entered into that freedom in 1896–7 with the adoption of a new constitution. Missionary workers at once rushed in, and the government even asked the Methodist presiding elder to organize national normal schools with foreign Protestants as the chief teachers.

At Callao, in Peru, was established a native congregation in charge of an agent of the Bible Society, **FRANCISCO PENZOTTI,** a humble Italian carpenter, who had been converted in Montevideo. Mobs tried to break up his work. At last Penzotti was imprisoned, shut up with a hundred criminals of all kinds in a foul, half-subterranean jail, and kept there for eight months while his church maintained its meetings and prayed for the spiritual redemption of Peru.

In 1895 two young Englishmen, **J. L. JARRETT** and **F. J. PETERS,** went to Cuzco and began a mission, but were at once banished. They compelled the government to give an indemnity, and reëstablished the mission.

Lima, one of the cities of the old inquisition, is also the seat of America's oldest university, that existed before the first settlers reached Jamestown or Plymouth. In Lima, however, is an educational work far more hopeful for South America — that of the Methodists, which has come up to a position of great influence after years of desperate struggle against the opposition of the Catholics.

COLOMBIA AND VENEZUELA, like the Inca country to the south, have proved the most difficult of mission fields, and only a beginning has been made there. Colombia's thick forests, with the great herds of cattle in both countries, constitute their wealth; but these republics are little developed.

The first permanent mission in South America was established by the Northern Presbyterians in 1856 at Bogota, by **REV. HORACE B. PRATT,** and ever since the Presbyterians, with the Bible Society, have been practically the only agents in the work. The bitter opposition of the priests and the apathy and religious indifference of the people continue to hold back the gospel. At one time the priests of Medillin got rich Catholics to visit the parents that were sending their children to the Protestant school, and offered free books, food, clothing, and tuition if they would send them to the Catholic school and sign a paper promising no longer to support the Protestants!

A consecrated layman, **ADAM ERWIN,** with a brave heart in a dwarfed and crippled body, laid the foundation for the work in Barranquilla. Unsupported by any board, he stayed alone for years. "God opened the way for me to come," he said, "but He has never opened it for me to go away." He won a great influence, and when he died, past the age of eighty, one of the priests said, "Mr. Erwin was truly a good man; the only wrong thing about him was his religion."

The first church in Venezuela was established through the bravery of an orphan from Spain, **EMILIO SILVA**

BRYANT, who, at the age of eighteen, went to Caracas in 1884 with his foster father. He was a humble manual laborer and stricken with consumption, and his little band of believers were compelled to worship in closest secrecy, but he held them together until the missionaries could form them into a regularly constituted church.

In 1897 the Presbyterians sent to Caracas REV. T. S. POND, and the Christian Alliance also has begun work there, together with the South American Evangelical Mission of Toronto and the Venezuela Mission, especially formed for labors in this neglected land.

XV.

CENTRAL AMERICA

CENTRAL AMERICA presents essentially the same missionary problem as South America and Mexico. Its five republics, together with British Honduras, have an area of about 200,000 square miles, equalling four States of New York. Its population is three and a half million, equalling that of the city of New York. Like Mexico, it includes the climate and plants of all zones.

Guatemala is the largest and most populous of these republics, Honduras the most rich in minerals, Salvador the most dense in population; Costa Rica (" Rich Coast") leads in agriculture and in the wealth and enterprise of its people ; Nicaragua is noted for its lake, which is the largest body of fresh water between Lake Michigan and Lake Titicaca. In Central America, contrary to the experience of other lands, the Indian type is not dying out, but is growing stronger, and the European element is diminishing and seems likely to pass away altogether.

Central America has free schools, but only a very small part of its population is educated. It has religious freedom, but its Catholicism is shamefully degraded, and the Indians in many places hide, under the altars in the churches, dolls representing their old pagan gods, and so worship both deities at once.

THE MORAVIANS have the largest mission in Central America. Having begun in 1848, they labor on the Mosquito or eastern coast of Nicaragua, and have practically evangelized the entire tribe of 10,000 Indians who live there.   The English Wesleyans began work in 1825 in British Honduras, and have branched out into Guatemala.   The British and American Bible Societies make these republics a field for their useful toil, the American forces being under the lead of that hero of South America, Penzotti.   The Central American Mission, which was founded in 1890, works among the Spanish-speaking inhabitants of all the republics.   The Seventh-Day Adventists have two missions, one in the north and the other in the south of the country.   The Northern Presbyterian mission in Guatemala was established in 1882 on the invitation of President Barrios, who, after breaking the power of the Jesuits and confiscating their property, visited the United States.   The first missionary was Rev. John C. Hill, and Barrios paid his travelling expenses and bought his church and school equipment.

XVI.

MEXICO

MEXICO, with a territory about one-fourth that of the United States, has a population of twelve and a half million. More than a third of these are Indians, descendants of the proud ancient race of Aztecs. They have furnished some of the most prominent men in Mexican politics. They are almost untouched by the missionaries, and Catholicism has not lifted them above their old-time paganism. The Aztecs in Chiquatal walked for miles over the mountains to beg Mr. Haywood, the Methodist missionary, to establish a school for them.

Nearly half the people are Mestizos, mixed white and Indian, and most of the remainder are pure Spaniards, with English, German, and American elements in the population. From the tropics of the coast to the cold mountain regions, all climates and vegetations are met in Mexico, which is among the most delightful of lands. Its wealth of iron, gold, and silver is seemingly inexhaustible. Its historic remains, especially the ruined cities of Yucatan, are full of romance. The University of Mexico was established eighty-three years before Harvard.

A greatly degraded Catholicism is the religion of the people, more than 99 per cent of them belonging to that church. They are divided between two rival Marys,

"Our Lady of Guadalupe" and the "Virgin of Reme-
dios." In 1857 religious liberty was granted; monastic
institutions are forbidden; there can be no religious
teaching in the public schools, and public ceremonies are
never opened with prayer. Since 1884, under the
peaceful and enlightened administration of President
Diaz, the country has enjoyed great prosperity.

MELINDA RANKIN was the pioneer missionary to
Mexico, though we must not forget that the American
army carried with it the Bible in the Mexican War, and
introduced it to the people, who proved hungry for its
truths, while the American Bible Society followed with
its blessed work of Bible distribution. Miss Rankin had
been teaching a mission school at Brownsville, Texas,
but in 1866 she established at Monterey a Christian
school, from which a noble influence radiated far and
wide. She raised money herself and sent out Bible dis-
tributors, and kept up this noble work for twenty years.

As one result of her work, at Ville de Cos, a mining
town in the state of Zacetecas, the Mexicans that had
received the good news formed a primitive church which
met secretly in a private house to read the Bible. After
the establishment of religious liberty they came out
openly, appointed one of their own number to serve as
pastor, and by 1872 had built themselves a church.

REV. HENRY C. RILEY, turned to Mexico through Miss
Rankin's influence, went to the capital in 1869, bought
church property, and joined himself to an eloquent
priest, Francisco Aguilas, who had renounced the cor-
ruptions of Catholicism. Another able priest, Manuel
Aguas, set out to refute Aguilas, but in the process converted himself. The result was the founding of the

" Church of Jesus," which has since come under the care of the Episcopal Church, and is a part of its mission in Mexico. More than forty Protestants lost their lives in the disturbances caused by these events.

Persecution was common in those early days, and Protestant missions in Mexico number in all sixty-five martyrs. The pioneer missionary of the American Board, Rev. J. L. Stephens, sent to the state of Jalisco in 1872, was assassinated, together with one of his converts, by a mob aroused by a Catholic priest. Six Presbyterians were killed at Acapulco.

Abraham Gomez, just ordained to the Protestant ministry at Ahuacualtitlan, was beaten to death with his Bible, which his murderers then laid beneath his head for a pillow. At El Carro the Catholics stoned to death Gregoria Monreal, and then cut off his head.

Rev. John O. Westrup, pioneer missionary of the Southern Baptists, was murdered in 1880 by a band of Mexicans and Indians. Rev. W. D. Powell succeeded him, was driven out of his places of worship, attempts were made on his life, and on one of his evangelistic tours he was attacked by a highwayman, who, on discovering how little he had, offered to lend him money enough to get home!

PROTESTANT MISSIONS in Mexico are, as is natural, conducted almost entirely from the United States. The years from 1870 to 1874 saw the beginning of most of these enterprises. In 1873 the Methodists' pioneer in India, William Butler, became their pioneer in Mexico. He obtained for his mission in Puebla the building that had been used by the inquisition, and in the City of Mexico the great monastery of St. Francis, where four thousand monks had lived, but only fourteen were living there at the time of its confiscation by the government. It is on the very site of Montezuma's palace.

The Baptist Home Mission Society had arrived in 1870, the Friends in 1871, and then followed closely the American Board, the Presbyterians North and South, Methodists North and South, Baptists South, Reformed Presbyterians South, Cumberland Presbyterians, Seventh Day Adventists, and Christians. These various societies labor in admirable fellowship and co-operation. Eight of them publish excellent periodicals, and the mission presses, especially the important houses of the Methodists and Presbyterians, have scattered at least 200,000,000 pages of religious literature.

XVII.

THE WEST INDIES

THE MORAVIANS sent their first missionaries to the Danish West Indies. A negro called Antony, at the court of Christian VI., King of Denmark, told Count Zinzendorf about the miseries of the negro slaves in the island of St. Thomas. When he heard of it, a young Moravian, Leonard Dober, declared that he would go to preach Christ to those slaves, though he had to become a slave like them.

On December 13, 1732, having overcome much opposition, Dober reached St. Thomas, accompanied by his friend David Nitschman, whose trade as a carpenter was their support until Nitschman's return the next April. They had started out with only a little more than $3 apiece. Dober was a potter, but could not find the proper clay, so that he lived upon work of all kinds precariously obtained, and supported life on bread and water, spending most of his time teaching the negro slaves upon the plantations.

In November, 1733, Dober was encouraged by the arrival of fourteen men and four women who had crossed the Atlantic in a room below the second deck, only ten feet square, and so low that they could not even sit upright, but had to lie on the floor. The voyage lasted more than half a year, and they suffered greatly.

Numbers of them perished from the effects of the

climate. The survivors were imprisoned by the enemies of the mission, and were only released through the personal efforts of Count Zinzendorf, who crossed the Atlantic to visit the mission. In the meantime, the negroes continued to hold meetings by themselves, and would come in great numbers, singing and praying under the prison windows. It was during this visit that Zinzendorf composed his famous hymn, "Jesus, Thy blood and righteousness."

Within seventeen years nearly fifty Moravian missionaries died in the Danish West Indies, and 127 within 50 years; but their labors won the hearts both of the black men and their owners, and as fast as the brethren fell, others were ready to take their places. Droughts, hurricanes, fires, negro insurrections, sickness, and famines interfered with the work of the missionaries, but they never faltered.

Their labors spread to the other Danish islands, Santa Cruz and St. John. They were invited by the English to send missionaries to Jamaica, and soon won great influence over the slaves. An aged woman walked eleven miles to attend gospel meetings. "Love makes the way short," she explained. When the English emancipated the slaves (in 1834–38), there were nearly 2,000 Christian negroes who, clothed all in white, held a thanksgiving service at the mission church.

In similar ways the Moravians were the pioneers in preaching to the blacks of St. Christopher's; of Antigua, where the slaves were freed four years before the time set by Parliament, largely owing to the good work of the Moravian missionaries; in Barbados, that island more thickly inhabited than China, where the first English clergyman who taught the blacks was indicted for the offence; and in Tobago, thought by many to be Robin-son Crusoe's island. For the first century the mission-aries died at the average rate of two a year.

The Moravians still conduct missions in these eastern islands, and also in Jamaica.

THOMAS COKE, the large-minded organizer of Metho-dist missions, was the principal agent in introducing that church into the West Indies. During his laborious life he made nine voyages to America, and nearly all of them in-cluded visits of preaching and investiga-tion among those islands.

His personal safety was often menaced. His missionaries were thrust into prison. Sometimes the negro slaves were severely flogged for attending a prayer meeting. On St. Eustatius a law was passed that a slave should be whipped every time he was found praying, while a white person convicted of praying with his brethren was, on the third offence, to be whipped and banished from the island, his goods being confiscated. Harry, a slave preacher of much power, was unmercifully beaten, imprisoned, and banished so secretly that for ten years no one knew his whereabouts, Dr. Coke afterwards finding him in the United States. In Jamaica, when a band of revellers were mocking the gospel meet-ings, a young actress, who had been shouting out her pretended " experiences," fell down dead — a tragic event that had a most salutary effect.

With great industry in the way of raising money, and with great personal courage and faith, Dr. Coke was instrumental in planting gospel missions over the larger part of the archipelago.

IN CUBA AND PORTO RICO many denominations in the United States have established missions, Cuba especially having as a notable part of its history the labors of that earnest worker, Dr. Alberto J. Diaz. The work in these islands, however, is to be considered more appropriately in a volume devoted to home missions.

IN HAITI AND SAN DOMINGO the Episcopal Church has a strong mission. These two negro republics, occupying that beautiful island which was the first to be colonized by Spain, speak French (Haiti) and Spanish (San Domingo), and are held firmly under the sway of Catholicism. The Christian Alliance labors in San Domingo and Jamaica, and in Jamaica the Friends have one of their earliest and strongest missions. The Presbyterian Church in Canada has an interesting work in Trinidad.

The terrible superstition of voodooism has a strong hold upon the negroes of the West Indies. Impurity is a common sin — more than sixty per cent of the negroes in Jamaica are said to be of illegitimate birth. Nevertheless, when really reached by the gospel, they make true Christians, warm-hearted and sincere.

XVIII.

GREENLAND

HANS EGEDE was the noble pioneer missionary to Greenland. He was a young Norwegian clergyman, and became strongly moved by the story of the sorrowful plight of the natives of Greenland, terribly degraded, and shut off from the gospel by the fearful difficulties of travel in those days.

About the year 1000 A. D., the Greenlanders were converted to Christianity by the Norwegians, and the names of a

EGEDE

series of bishops have come down to us, who ruled the church on the east coast down to 1406. But this colony of Christians was destroyed by wild hordes of Skrellings, and to this day the eastern shore of Greenland is mainly a desolate, icy solitude.

For thirteen years Egede prayed and planned for a mission to Greenland, meeting with a storm of ridicule and opposition, and being almost dissuaded by the tearful entreaties of his wife, who afterward became his most zealous helper in the work. The story of those thirteen years of patient endeavor to arouse men's consciences to missionary effort is among the most pathetic in all missionary annals.

At last, on May 3, 1721, Egede set sail in the Hope,

under the patronage of Frederick IV., King of Denmark. Good Hope was the name he gave to his colony in Greenland. With extreme difficulty, and after three years of toil, Egede learned the language. He would get his little boy to draw pictures illustrating gospel scenes, and as the natives asked questions about them, he would both gain new insight into their language and give them new insight into the truth.

There came the pinch of hunger and disease. The natives held cruelly aloof. His followers mutinied. Egede's heroic wife shamed them to constancy. Just in the nick of time she discovered on the horizon the ship bringing supplies and fresh courage. It was with great joy, on New Year's Day, 1725, that the first convert was baptized, — Frederic Christian, who afterward became a teacher among the natives.

MATTHEW STACH and CHRISTIAN STACH, cousins, were the Moravian pioneers in Greenland. They belonged to that band who, under the lead of Christian David, fled from Catholic persecution to the estate of the noble Count Zinzendorf in Saxony and built the settlement of Herrnhut.

A negro from the West Indies stirred their zeal by relating the sufferings of the slaves there, and two of their number made public their resolution to carry the gospel to them, and to become slaves themselves, if necessary, to get the opportunity to preach to them. There were only 600 persons then at Herrnhut, yet within ten years missionaries had gone thence to all quarters of the globe.

Among the very first of these, in 1733, the Stachs set

forth, with Christian David, to Greenland. Daringly trusting Christ, they took "nothing for their journey." Their simple wants were marvellously supplied. Egede received them with heartiness. They built a cabin and called the place New Herrnhut. Frederic Boenish and John Beck came the next year. Unused to that stern coast, and almost entirely destitute, it was with extreme difficulty that they preserved themselves alive. A fearful plague of smallpox came, through which they nursed many of the terrified natives. A strange disease settled upon them, and they nearly lost the use of their limbs.

They were unlearned men, and the language is one of tremendous difficulty. Take for a sample the word "savigeksiniariartokasuaromaryotittogog," which means, "He says you will also go away quickly in like manner and buy a pretty knife." One year the annual ship brought them no supplies from Europe, and they almost starved. Train oil was a delicacy. They even ate old tallow candles and raw seaweed. The natives were stupid, unappreciative, and cruel. The missionaries were mocked, insulted, pelted with stones, threatened with death. It was five years before they won a single convert — the noble Kayarnak, who was baptized on Easter Sunday, March 29, 1739. It was 1747 before they could build their first church. It was 1758 before they could establish the new settlement of Lichtenfels to the south. Nevertheless the Moravians persevered cheerfully amid countless obstacles, until now, through their labor and that of the Danes, Greenland is a Christian country, redeemed from a condition of filthy, ignorant, cruel savagery, to the light and beauty of a Christian civilization.

XIX.

EUROPE

GREECE

JONAS KING, the first and the greatest of Protestant missionaries to Greece, went there in 1828 with American relief for the suffering patriots fighting for their independence against the Turks. He had grown up in a godly Massachusetts home, being led by his father to read the Bible through every year. He learned the English grammar while hoeing corn, read the twelve books of the Æneid in fifty-eight days, and became after graduation a professor at Amherst.

His distribution of food and clothing opened the hearts of the Greeks to his preaching, and till his death in 1869, at the age of seventy-seven, Dr. King was a power in Greece. He labored chiefly at Athens, where he raised up several generations of Greek Protestant preachers and teachers.

The Greek church threatened his patrons with excommunication. They haled him before the Areopagus. Fifty men bound themselves together to kill him. A mob assailed his house, and he was saved only by unfurling the American flag. He was imprisoned in a loathsome jail, and exiled from the country, but restored on demand of the United States government. He was anathematized by the " Holy Synod of Athens "; but he kept right on with his work.

He knew eleven languages and could speak fluently in five. The Greek Protestant church, formed after plans drawn up by Dr. King, has sole direction now of Protestant work in the kingdom. Its leading member is Dr. Kalopothakes, who was converted by the Southern Presbyterian missionaries, Samuel R. Houston and G. W. Leyburn, in a school they established in Sparta. He became Dr. King's assistant, and for nearly thirty years edited the Protestant paper, *The Star of the East.*

Besides this Presbyterian work, the Baptists have conducted a mission in

—1721. Egede.
—1733. Stach.

(*Carey in India.*) 1793—
(*The Duff sails.*) 1796—

(*Morrison in China.*) 1807—

(*Judson in Burma.*) 1813—

(*Fisk in Syria.*) 1819—

(*Gutzlaff in Siam.*) 1828—
                    —1828. King.
                    —1830. Robertson.
                                Hill.
(*Goodell in Turkey.*) 1831—
                    —1832. Chase.
(*Perkins in Persia.*) 1833—
                    —1834. Sears.
                                Oncken

(*Gardiner in South
      America.*) 1838—

                    —1844. Nast.

                    —1849. Jacoby.

                    —1853. Petersen.
                                Larsson.
                    —1855. Wiberg.
                    —1857. Prettyman.
                                Long.
                                Willerup.
(*Williams in Japan.*) 1859—

                    —1870. Cote.
                    —1871. Vernon.
                    —1872. Clark.
                                McAll.
                                Gulick.
                    —1873. Taylor.

                    —1883. Methodists in Finland.
(*Allen in Korea.*) 1884—

                    —1887. Baptists in Russia.
                    —1889. Burt.

AMERICAN MISSIONS IN EUROPE.

Greece, which is now discontinued; and the Episcopal church, since 1830 when it sent out J. J. Robertson and J. H. Hill, has conducted a successful educational mission, whose standing monument is the fine girls' school at Athens.

BULGARIA

THE METHODIST WORK in Bulgaria lies north of the Balkan Mountains. The Congregational work to the south of those mountains is mentioned under Turkey. In 1857 the Methodists sent to Bulgaria Rev. Wesley Prettyman and Rev. Albert L. Long. Shumla and Tirnova became the centres of work.

The Catholics warned their followers away from Protestant preaching on pain of excommunication. A Bulgarian priest came with tears to Dr. Long to ask the loan of a Bible which his superior had forbidden him to read. Elieff, the first convert, had got hold of a New Testament, and did not know that a single person in all the world had the joy he discovered in it. He became Dr. Long's colporteur and assistant.

The picturesque event of the mission was its introduction to the Molokans. In the seventeenth century two young Russians, going to England, had returned with a purer religion. They taught their friends to reject image-worship and other superstitions, and a church of a million people grew up, called Molokans from the Russian *moloko*, milk, because they drank milk on fast days. They gladly welcomed the Methodists, and the first Russian Methodist church was built at Tultcha.

During the war between Russia and Turkey, the Methodist missions suffered, but they have recovered ground.

The American Girls' School at Loftcha is now the most hopeful feature of the work.

AUSTRIA

THE AMERICAN BOARD established its mission to Austria in 1872, the pioneers being H. A. Schauffler, E. A. Adams, Albert W. Clark, and E. C. Bissell; Dr. Clark is still at the head of the mission. The centre of work is Prague, and the chief effort is made among the Bohemians, who are even followed into Russia. There are thirteen flourishing churches, that at Prague, the mother church, being in charge of Rev. Alvis Adlof, a most able man, who quietly told the people that he was ready to serve them for no fixed salary but for whatever God led them to give in their weekly offerings.

All these Congregational churches must be conducted under the legal guise of private parties, with the congregation as invited guests. As the first missionaries, on entering this land of John Huss, drew near to Prague in the railroad train, they sung " Praise God from whom all blessings flow"; and their labors have been full of blessings to the land. Persecutions have been many and fierce. Within a year a young shoemaker, for example, has been imprisoned for distributing Christian literature, and had a good time preaching Christ to the other prisoners.

The work for women has its climax in the Krabchitz Seminary, "the Mount Holyoke of Bohemia." Among the most active workers for Bohemian women is the first convert of the mission, Miss Julia Most.

THE NORTHERN BAPTISTS also have a work in Prague, in Vienna, in Hungary, and Galicia. The church at Prague was established in 1885, with sixteen members. It now has two hundred and ten, of whom about one hundred and seventy were born Catholics. A Bohemian Baptist paper is also published.

ITALY

THE METHODIST MISSION to Italy was established in 1871 by Dr. Leroy M. Vernon, who was succeeded in 1889 by Dr. William Burt. Methodist churches sprung from this mission are scattered up and down Italy, but the centre of the work is at Rome, where the mission has built a handsome edifice that fitly represents Protestant Christianity in the midst of the architectural monuments that surround it. The mission carries on a well-equipped publishing house, and conducts a very successful girls' school and a young women's college, Crandon Hall, chiefly patronized by Catholic parents.

It is said that the first person to enter Rome through the breach in the walls made by Garibaldi's cannon, was a colporteur with his pack of Bibles. Ever since, the government has allowed perfect liberty to Protestant teaching. Indeed, when Garibaldi and Victor Emmanuel were besieging Rome, the Pope and his cardinals deposited the immense treasures of the Vatican for safe-keeping not with a member of their own church, but with a Lutheran banker! At the beginning of the kingdom of United Italy about eighty per cent of the people were illiterate; now, less than thirty-five per cent. The Italians are learning that the Protestants are not the evil folk described by their priests, and slowly but surely a more enlightened religion is gaining ground among them.

SOUTHERN BAPTIST missions in Italy were established in 1870, by William N. Cote, M. D., who was the first missionary to enter Rome after the army of Victor Emmanuel had thrown open the gates to the gospel. "Go on with your work," said a city guard to the colporteur; "Rome has need of these books."

On January 30 of the next year the first church was organized. The work began to spread to other cities. In 1873, Dr. George B. Taylor was placed at the head of the mission, and has filled the post with great power ever since. An important step was the establishment, in 1878, of a mission home in Rome, an excellent building near the Pantheon and the University. Another forward step was the establishment, in 1884, of the Baptist paper, *Il Testimonio*.

The work has extended, though in the midst of much persecution from the Catholics, through Sardinia, Tuscany, south-eastern Italy, the western Riviera, and the Waldensian valleys in the north. There is a theological seminary at Rome. In several places whole villages have rebelled against the priests, driven them out, and gone over to Protestantism.

FRANCE

ROBERT WHITAKER McALL was an English Congregational clergyman who went to Paris on a visit, and was moved to pity by the condition of the godless people there. In January, 1872, a few months after the fall of the Commune, he with his noble wife quietly began work in a part of Paris crowded with desperate communists. When he began his work, he knew only two sentences of French : "God loves you," and "I love you."

He offered a free religion, a decided novelty in that land of priestly extortion. Mr. and Mrs. McAll always served at their own charges. The McAll missions are rented halls, managed most economically, and most of their workers labor without salaries. They co-operate with all other evangelical forces, and send their converts into the regularly formed Protestant churches, so that the McAll mission is a help to all kinds of gospel work.

McALL

Dr. McAll received two gold medals from learned societies, and had the satisfaction of seeing his enterprise, born of pure faith, become the greatest of all agencies for the salvation of France. He passed away in 1894, his successor being Rev. Charles E. Greig. There are about a hundred McAll missions in France, and their support comes chiefly from Great Britain and the United States.

NORTHERN BAPTIST work in France was begun in 1832 by Professor Irah Chase, the first permanent missionary being Rev. Isaac Willmarth, who organized the first Baptist church in Paris in 1835. There was great persecution until the French Revolution brought religious liberty, and even then the pastor of the first church in Paris, with others, was thrown into prison and fined. There are thirty churches, many of them in southeastern France and in the French-speaking part of Switzerland, and all the work is carried on by Frenchmen.

SPAIN

SPAIN possesses sixty-five Catholic cathedrals and thirty thousand Catholic churches, convents, and the like, yet it sadly needs Protestantism, for not half of the eighteen million people can read and write, and all of them are bound by the shackles of superstition. To the earlier bigotry and religious fanaticism are succeeding atheism and religious indifference.

The Northern Baptists in 1870 took up the work of Professor W. J. Knapp in Madrid. Their mission has passed through great trials, but they have now four churches, the work centering in Barcelona.

The American Board mission to Spain was established in 1872, and in spite of great persecution has done a noble work, having now eight churches and sixteen schools. The chief success is the American school for girls carried on by Rev. W. H. Gulick and his wife. It was a great triumph when the girls from this school were the first of Spanish womanhood to win admission to the University at Madrid, carrying off at once the highest honors. When, at the outbreak of our war with Spain, the school moved across the border to Biarritz, France, the scholars gladly moved with it, and soon the mission will return, taking up its abode at Madrid.

GERMANY

BAPTIST WORK in Germany had its virtual start in 1834, when at midnight Dr. Barnas Sears rowed in a small boat with seven converts to a point several miles from the city of Hamburg, and there baptized them. Among these was Johann Gerard Oncken, who became the founder and apostle of Baptist churches throughout central Europe. In 1859 twelve young men, who had been taught in Hamburg, were ordained in a single day to the Baptist ministry. A large publishing house at Cassel and a theological seminary in Hamburg are important centres of the work, and Baptist churches are now found in all the leading cities.

ONCKEN

WILLIAM NAST was the founder of German Methodism, not only in America, but in his homeland. At the University of Tübingen his religion was spoiled by philosophy. When professor of German at West Point he became a hearty Methodist, and at once entered upon a ministry to his countrymen in the United States.

In 1844 he was sent to Germany to prospect for a mission, finding the way prepared in advance by the work of a Mr. Müller, who had become a Methodist in England, whither he had gone to avoid service in Bonaparte's army. His meetings were so crowded that there was no room for kneeling.

LUDWIG S. JACOBY, M. D., a German boy who was one of Nast's converts in America, was sent out in 1849 as the first missionary. He got a public hall at Bremen. It was soon packed with a crowd of four hundred. He soon moved into and packed a hall twice as large. *Der Evangelist* was established, the pioneer of a wide seed-sowing through books and papers.

JACOBY

REV. LOUIS NIPPERT, sent out in 1850, had to preach his first sermon in a barn, horses and pigs, bellowing cows and cackling hens contesting with him the ears of his audience. Sunday schools were introduced. In one place a watch-night meeting, held below while a ball was going on above, came out the victor; the ball was abandoned, the dancers crowded the gospel meeting, and God's power was shown in many hearts.

There was much persecution. Drunken mobs attacked Methodist chapels. One colporteur was seized, his clothes torn off, and he thrown into a ditch. In one prison a Methodist preacher found three infidels, he put in jail for praying too much, and they for praying too little! Nevertheless, the cause prospered. The Martin Mission Institute has grown up at Frankfort-on-the-Main. A book concern is in vigorous operation. A remarkable deaconess movement has been set on foot. There are fifty-five Methodist churches in north Germany, and eighty-four in south Germany.

METHODIST MISSIONS in Switzerland are an offshoot from the flourishing work in Germany. Two German preachers started the work in 1856, and in 1886 it was set off as a separate mission. One of the early preachers went to Zurich, advertised a service, and when the time came not a soul entered the hall. The next Sunday he had five hearers, the next Sunday seven; but in the evening his perseverance was rewarded, for his congregation filled the place. Zurich is now a strong Methodist centre, with more than two thousand Sunday-school scholars, and a large society for spreading Christian literature. There are forty-nine Methodist churches in Switzerland

NORWAY

METHODIST WORK for Scandinavia began in New York City. Olof Gustaf Hedstrom, a Swedish tailor, was converted in 1829, and became a zealous preacher. A ship was bought named the John Wesley, and stationed at a pier in the North River for a sailors' bethel. The many converts made at this mission and in the West wrote letters home, and visited the homeland. In 1853 Rev. O. P. Petersen was sent back home "to raise up a people for God in Norway." There was much opposition from the state

PETERSEN   church, but revivals came, a paper, *Kristelig Tidende*, was started, a publishing house and deaconess work were established, and now there are forty-seven churches.

SWEDEN

METHODIST missions in Sweden were established in 1853 by J. P. Larsson, a Swede who was converted in New York, and returned home to preach the new-found gospel to his friends. The first church, at Carlskrona, was built as the result of great sacrifice, many of the people living on two meals a day, and others pawning clothing and furniture in order to give. In 1874 the king granted graciously a petition signed by fourteen hundred Methodists, asking to be set apart from the state church as a separate institution. Like all Protestant work in Europe, the Swedish churches lose greatly because of immigration to the United States, but there are one hundred and thirty-two churches in all, with the enthusiastic beginning of a home missionary society.

BAPTIST MISSIONS in Sweden were established in 1855, and now number nearly six hundred churches. The real beginning was in the days when Baptist preachers were forbidden to preach openly in that country; but Rev. A. Wiberg was so faithful in the circulation of literature that when freedom of preaching was given, churches of the Baptist faith sprung up everywhere. Now the Baptist churches, though compelled by the peculiar laws of the land to form a nominal part of the state church, are free from the persecution to which they were formerly subjected. The Baptists have a theological seminary at Stockholm, and under their influence a strong Baptist movement has been established in Norway, Finland, and Denmark.

DENMARK

METHODIST missions in Denmark were an outgrowth of the work in Norway, and were commenced by Rev. C. Willerup, a Dane who had been preaching in Wisconsin and then in Norway. Beginning in 1857, he soon felt the great need of a church building. A convert proposed a gift that astonished all Scandinavia — $1,500 toward such a building. This was a stimulus for other goodly gifts, and other chapels were built. There are now twenty-four Methodist churches in Denmark.

The Disciples of Christ and the Seventh Day Adventists also carry on work in these three Scandinavian countries, the former having sixteen churches, and the latter sixty-nine.

RUSSIA

THE BAPTIST MISSIONS in Russia, established in 1887, began with German emigrants in the southeastern part of the country. These Baptists have suffered severe persecutions. Families have been torn apart, the children placed in Greek nunneries or monasteries, the parents exiled to Siberia. Whole churches have been transported in a body. One church, greatly persecuted, sold its property and went to South America. Many have been compelled to flee to central Europe. In spite of all this, however, and even because of it, the Baptist churches in Russia continue to grow in numbers and power.

IN FINLAND the work of the Methodists was begun in 1883 by a preacher from Sweden, and in 1892 the country was set off as a separate mission. There are seven churches, nearly all in Finland, though there is the beginning of a work in St. Petersburg. There is a theological seminary, and there are two monthly papers.

XX.

AFRICA

AFRICA, under the blaze of the equatorial sun, is yet the "Dark Continent" as concerns Christian civilization. Nowhere else are the masses so degraded. And yet they are, in the main, a warm-hearted, affectionate people, capable of receiving the loftiest ideas of our religion, and embodying them in apostolic lives. Only the borders, practically, of this vast region have been touched by the gospel, and it is only during recent decades that African missions have been pushed on any extensive and widely effective scale; but already there is promise of gospel triumphs equal to any won in the world.

THE FIELD is an enormous one — an area equal to Europe and North America put together — a vast continent five thousand miles long and nearly five thousand miles broad, and with a population about twice as large as that of the United States. To meet the spiritual needs of this great number of people, there is in Africa about one missionary to every 50,000 souls, counting as missionaries the lay workers also and the wives of the missionaries; while in the United States, not counting lay workers or ministers' wives, we have one minister to every 500 persons.

THE DIFFICULTIES in the way of evangelizing this

greatest of all mission fields are all but insuperable. The absence of harbors, roads, and navigable streams renders Africa the most inaccessible region of the globe. The appalling number of languages — 438, with 1,153 dialects besides — is a formidable barrier to intercourse with the natives. About a third of Africa is Mohammedan — the most difficult of all religions to dislodge. A still greater impediment to missionary enterprise is the climate, which is the most unhealthy in the world. Africa is the graveyard of missionaries. About one hundred missionary societies are now working in Africa. Mr. Taylor, in his "Price of

1737. Schmidt.

1742. Willem, first convert

(*Carey in India.*) 1793—

1799. Vanderkemp.

(*Morrison in China.*) 1807—

(*Judson in Burma.*) 1813—

1817. Moffat.
1818. Jones.
       Bevan.

(*Fisk in Syria.*) 1819—

1821. Lott Carey.

(*Gutzlaff in Siam.*) 1828—
(*King in Greece.*)

1830. Gobat.

(*Goodell in Turkey.*) 1831—
(*Perkins in Persia.*) 1833—

1833. Cox.
1834. Wilson.
       Seys.
1835. Missionaries driven
       from Madagascar.

1837. Payne.
(*Gardiner in South America.*) 1838—   1838. Krapf.

1841. Crowther.
       Livingstone.

1850. Bowen.

(*Williams in Japan.*) 1859—

1861. Religious liberty in
       Madagascar.

1876. Mackay.

1882. Good.

(*Allen in Korea.*) 1884—   1884. Taylor.
1885. Hannington.

1888. Parker.

1890. Pilkington.

1895. French conquest
       of Madagascar.

GREAT MISSIONARIES
TO AFRICA.

Africa," takes only seven of these — all American societies — and gives a list of 190 of their missionaries that
have perished in the Dark Continent, chiefly from the
ravages of the dreaded fever.

THE HORRORS OF THE SLAVE TRADE are passing
away, but " Christian " civilization is replacing them with
still greater horrors, with its unspeakably iniquitous traffic
in strong drink.   Intemperance, ruinous in Europe and
America, becomes insanity and swift death under a tropical
sun.   It is estimated that 40,000,000 Africans have been
sold into slavery.   The rum trade will soon be the cause
of the death, spiritual and physical, of more than that
number of Africans.   The record at Madeira of liquor
bound for Africa during a single week was 28,000 cases
of whiskey, 30,000 cases of brandy, 30,000 cases of Old
Tom, 36,000 barrels of rum, 800,000 demijohns of rum,
24,000 butts of rum, 15,000 barrels of absinthe, and 960,-
000 cases of gin.   No hindrance to the progress of missions compares with this terrible curse that comes largely
from Christian America.

THE MAP OF AFRICA given herewith shows the " protectorates " and " spheres of influence " into which the
continent has been partitioned out among the European
powers, and indicates the regions where the great missionaries have labored, and also the centres of work of
our largest American societies.   We must bear in mind
that the map does not show the still more important work
done in Africa by the great missionary societies of England, Scotland, Germany, and France, though the following biographical sketches will indicate some of the centres
of their activity.

TURKISH (Independent)

TURKISH

BRITISH (Br.)

U.P.

SPANISH (Sp.)

FRENCH (Fr.)

ITALIAN

Gobat Fr.

Br.

ABYSSINIA

ITALIAN

Br.
Port.

Br.

Ger.

Br.

Crowther
Bowen
B.S

AME
Carey
Taylor
Cox Payne
U.B. Seys
BRITISH
M.N E L
LIBERIA

GERMAN (Ger.)

Niger

P.S
Guinness
BN
Richards
Taylor

Pilkington

Parker
Hannington

Krapf

S.e.
PN Wilson
Good

Madhas

CONGO
FREE
STATE
Tamkama
Livingstone

GERMAN

Congo Port.

C C
PORTUGUESE
(Port.)

PORTUGUESE

Zambesi

French

GERMAN

BRITISH

Moffat

Schmidt
Vanderkemp

American Missions.

BN--Baptist, North.
BS—Baptist, South.
C —Congregational.
CC —Canadian Congregational.
E—Episcopal
L —Lutheran.
MN —Methodist, North.
PN—Presbyterian, North.
PS—Presbyterian, South.
UB United Brethren.
UP —United Presbyterian.
The locations of other societies are
  given in the text.

AFRICA

PROTECTORATES
AND GREAT
MISSIONARIES.

GEORGE SCHMIDT, heroic Moravian, was the Protestant
pioneer missionary to Africa.   Ziegenbalg and Plutschau,
Danish pioneer missionaries to India, touched at the Cape
of Good Hope on their way east, and wrote home an appeal for missionaries to be sent to those neglected black
men.   Seven days after Schmidt heard of it, he was on
his way to offer himself for the task.   He was then only
twenty-seven years old, but had already spent six years in
a Bohemian prison for the sake of his Protestant faith,
and bore to his death marks of his chains.   As soon as
he was released from prison, he travelled about Europe
for a year, winning men to Christ.   He was a day laborer,
and had little education, but he was an apostle.   He
reached Cape Town July 9, 1737, and was received with
cruel scorn.   The Dutch hated the blacks, and despised
them.   The notice above one church door : " Hottentots
and dogs forbidden to enter ! " completely expresses
their attitude.   Schmidt was driven from place to place,
but succeeded in gathering around him a colony of
devoted Hottentots, who adored the first white man that
had ever treated them kindly.   Despairing of learning
their difficult language, with its clicks and other inhuman
sounds, he taught them Dutch, carrying on a well-attended
school and training the natives to habits of industry and
in the arts of civilization.   His first convert, Willem, was
baptized March 31, 1742, like Philip's Ethiopian, in a
stream by the way as they were journeying together, and
he became Schmidt's assistant — an honored and useful
man.   For six years the lonely missionary labored among
the Hottentots at the Cape, building up a congregation
of forty-seven persons ; but the Dutch at last sent him
back to Europe, where as a sexton and grave-digger he
lived to be seventy-six years old, praying every day for

South Africa, and dying at last, like Livingstone, on his knees.

JOHN THEODORE VANDERKEMP, of Holland, founded the South African mission of the London Missionary Society. He was fifty years old when he became a missionary. He was a man of great learning; was first a soldier and then a physician of much skill, becoming a director of a large hospital. He grew to be an infidel, but was aroused to a sense of his dangerous position by the sudden death by drowning of his wife and daughter, he himself barely escaping with his life. Out of his infidelity he won a simple-hearted, childlike faith, and an ardent zeal for the cause of his new-found Saviour that led him, soon after the formation of the London Missionary Society, to offer himself in their service. He sailed for Africa in December, 1798, on a convict transport, among whose wretched and mutinous passengers he did magnificent evangelistic work. Dr. Vanderkemp labored in South Africa till his death in 1811. His work was chiefly among the Hottentots, and it was interrupted by much grievous opposition from heathen chiefs and from the hostile Boers. He was compelled to move his Christian colony frequently, and often to protest against the cruelties inflicted upon the defenceless natives. In three years he himself spent $5,000 to redeem slaves from bondage. It was not till near the end of his life that the English finally conquered the Cape. Dr. Vanderkemp's last utterance, when asked, "Is it darkness or light with you?" was the single emphatic word, "Light!"

ROBERT MOFFAT, as Vanderkemp died, was growing up to take his place. He was an apprentice to a Scotch gardener, and began work at four o'clock on cold winter mornings, knocking his knuckles against his spade handle to keep them warm. A hard life, with little schooling, toughened his frame. Passing over a bridge one day he happened to see an announcement of a missionary meeting, which aroused memories of what his pious mother had told him of the heroic Moravian missionaries to Greenland and Labrador, and led to his offering himself to the London Missionary Society at the age of nineteen.

MOFFAT

He reached Cape Town on January 13, 1817. His destination was Namaqualand, north of the Orange River, the district controlled by a fierce chief named Africaner. The missionaries previously there had been compelled, through fear of him, to spend a week in a pit covered over, and then made good their escape. His conversion was reported, but the farmers on the way refused to believe the news and begged Moffat not to venture further.

The journey was a trying one over wastes of burning sands. One night, at the house of a wealthy Boer, the young missionary was conducting family prayers when he asked for the Hottentot servants to be brought in. " Hottentots ! " the man roared, " I will call my dogs and you may preach to them." Without a word Moffat began to read and explain the story of the Syrophenician woman, with her saying, " Even the dogs eat of the crumbs which fall from their master's table." " Hold ! " cried the Boer, " you shall have your Hottentots."

Africaner received him kindly, and became a noble Christian, gentle and true — one of the most conspicuous miracles of conversion in all history. With him, quite alone, Moffat lived and taught, being carpenter, smith, cooper, shoemaker, miller, baker, and housekeeper. Many were his trials, but they were all rewarded when he could take Africaner to Cape Town and exhibit him as a specimen of the marvels of God's grace.

Until 1870 Moffat, with Mary Moffat, his beautiful, heroic wife, labored in South Africa, preaching and translating, slowly winning the natives, making hazardous journeys of exploration. At one time, beset by hostile natives whose spears were levelled at him, the missionary threw open his breast and bade them strike. He won the day by his dauntlessness. His centre of labor was at Kuruman among the Bechuanas, into whose language he translated the entire Bible, the work of thirty years. "I felt it to be an awful thing," he said, "to translate the Book of God." He also established the mission in Matabeleland, farther north. His old age was passed in England, where he received many honors and a testimonial of $30,000, and where he died at the age of eighty-eight.

DAVID LIVINGSTONE, whom most men would place at the head of the great Protestant missionaries, was a poor

LIVINGSTONE

Scotch weaver's lad, born in 1813. With part of his first week's wages as "piecer boy," at a loom, he bought a Latin grammar, laying the rest of the money in his mother's lap.

By the age of nineteen he had decided to be a medical missionary, and after obtaining a most practical training, he reached South Africa in 1841 as a missionary of the London Society — a connection he maintained till 1856. He began with Moffat at Kuruman. "If you meet me down in the Colony," he wrote, " before eight years are expired, you may shoot me." It was there he married Mary Moffat, who made him a noble wife, and near there he had the famous fight with a lion, which bit through his arm bone.

Livingstone's chief work, to the outward eye, was exploration. With toil and peril such as only a heroic spirit and stout body could endure, he opened up the Zambesi country from ocean to ocean, and the region around the great African lakes, many of which he discovered. He became one with the natives, and obtained a marvellous ascendency over them — an influence steadily used to promote the cause of Christ. He was missionary above explorer, and explorer only because, as he said, " The end of the geographical feat is but the beginning of the missionary enterprise."

After leaving the London Society, he maintained his work by the sale of his books. With the exception of a brilliant visit to England in 1857, he buried himself in the Dark Continent. Stanley's search for him and his discovery of the aged and almost starving apostle in 1871 — an intercourse that was Stanley's spiritual birth — are well known to all.

The devoted man would not return to civilization, but continued his great work. On one of his latest journeys he read the Bible through four times. He grew more and more feeble; fainting, he had to be borne in a litter over miles of swamp; his men built him a rough hut, left him for the night, and in the morning of May 1, 1873, his loving black servant, Susi, found him on his knees by his bed, having passed away in the act of prayer. His faithful followers buried his heart under a tree, embalmed his body, and laboriously carried it a nine-month's jour-

ney to the coast, so that now it rests in Westminster
Abbey — the chief glory of that glorious shrine.

BAPTIST missions in Africa began with the sending out
in 1821 of Lott Carey, a slave who had bought his freedom.
He went to Liberia, and came to his death in 1828 while
engaged in a struggle against a slave-trader. In 1884
the American Baptists received from Rev. H. Grattan
Guinness, the English Baptist missionary, the mission he
had established on the Congo — a unique instance of the
transfer of a large and prosperous mission from one nation
to another. Since then the mission has flourished, especially during the wonderful revival under Rev. Henry
Richards, who, after preaching for six years without a
convert, received in a few years more than a thousand.
In a single year of this time he preached seven hundred
sermons — and the eager listeners would have them an
hour and a half long!

SAMUEL GOBAT, pioneer Protestant missionary to
Abyssinia, was a Swiss who began his work, in 1830, under the direction of the Church Missionary Society, and
labored in Abyssinia till 1836. His later years were spent
as Bishop of Jerusalem, where he died in 1879. He was
a man of great ability, speaking eight languages, of
devout piety, and of splendid courage and endurance.
Abyssinia is the only native Christian country in Africa,
and the only savage Christian country in the world. It
became Christian early in the fourth century under the
preaching of Frumentius, a boy of Tyre, who happened
to be captured, sold as a slave, and rose high in the royal
household, becoming tutor to the king's sons. Abyssinian
Christianity, however, is very corrupt.

JOHN LUDWIG KRAPF, a German, accomplished for northeast Africa much of what Livingstone wrought for central Africa. He began his labors in Abyssinia in 1838, and his work rapidly spread throughout all the region to the south. Under the Church Missionary Society he established his greatest mission, at Mombasa on the Zanzibar coast, from which he conducted extensive explorations, including Uganda and Mount Kenia. His researches in African languages were most fruitful also, and Bible translation in Germany occupied his closing years. He died in 1881, while on his knees in prayer.

MELVILLE B. COX, the first Methodist foreign missionary from the United States, volunteered to go to Africa,

COX

though he knew that he could not live long there. He asked of a friend that his epitaph should be, "Let a thousand fall before Africa is given up." He reached Liberia, the Methodist mission field in Africa, in 1833, and held under some evergreen palms the first African campmeeting. In five months the heroic man was seized by African fever and passed away.

JOHN SEYS had lived for many years in Trinidad, was fitted for the African climate, and felt himself impelled to take Cox's place, though five missionaries had passed away the year Cox died. He went out in 1834, and two hundred converts were made the first year. Ten thousand pagans came of their own accord to join the colony. Bishops Burns and Roberts were colored men successively set over this promising field, but in 1884 William Taylor was made first missionary bishop of Africa.

WILLIAM TAYLOR, "The Flaming Torch," as the Africans called him, was one of the greatest world evangelists since Paul. A wild youth, he became converted, and at once took to preaching. For seven years he was a street preacher in San Francisco. Then he became a mighty evangelist in the East, in Canada, England, Ireland, for four years doing a wonderful work in Australia. Then he made many hundreds of converts in South Africa; then he won thousands in the West Indies; next a thousand in Ceylon, and a thousand more in north

WILLIAM TAYLOR

and south India, where he established self-supporting churches; then to similar labors in South America, and finally to Africa, where for twelve years he toiled heroically to establish self-supporting stations, his missionaries earning their own support by farming and other labor — a method of work that has not proved very successful. This apostolic man, who for years slept with his head on a stone which he carried with him, and who, when asked for his address, said, "I am sojourning on the globe at present, but do not know how soon I shall be leaving," passed away at the age of eighty-one, in 1902. His successor is Bishop Hartzell, who oversees the flourishing Methodist missions in the Madeiras, Liberia, Angola (south of the Congo), and Rhodesia.

JOHN LEIGHTON WILSON is to be remembered as the missionary pioneer of the American Board in West Africa. In 1834 he established at Cape Palmas a mission in what is now Liberia. He explored the interior, making long journeys, mostly on foot, and he built up a flourishing Christian community. But the French occu-

pation caused the removal of his mission to the
Mpongwes, 1,200 miles south, on the Gaboon River,
where it is now under the control of the northern
Presbyterians. Failing health compelled Dr. Wilson to
return home, and he became, before the war, foreign
mission secretary of the Presbyterians, and during the
war, being a Southern man, he organized the foreign
work in the Southern Presbyterian Church and became
its secretary.

CONGREGATIONAL MISSIONS in Africa are now three,
— among the Zulus in Natal, and in Portuguese territory on the east and west coasts. The Zulu mission
was established in 1834, was greatly hindered by the
opposition of the Boers and of the treacherous Zulu king,
Dingaan, and by the war between Boers and Zulus. It
was ten years before the missionaries gained their first
convert — an old woman. Now the mission flourishes in
every way gloriously. The other two missions are later
— the western, 1880; the eastern, 1883.

THE NORTHERN PRESBYTERIAN mission in Africa
lies in the region around the mouth of the Gaboon River
on the West Coast. It was established in 1842, and has
cost the lives of many heroes, slain by the terrible West
Coast fever.

ADOLPHUS C. GOOD was one of these. He was a
poor lad, belonging "to the Grand Order of Log-
Cabin Men of America, where Lincoln belonged, and
Grant, and Garfield." He urged his sturdy health as one
reason why he should be appointed a missionary to the
deadly African station, and set sail in 1882. Ten missionaries were compelled to leave for home the first year,

and he was the only man left — and only twenty-six years old. Within ten months he could preach in the native tongue. His most conspicuous work — though he was an untiring evangelist and an orator scarcely second to Duff — was the exploration of the inland regions back from the station. Under terrible difficulties he journeyed many hundreds of miles through a country never before visited by a white man.

GOOD

One indication of Dr. Good's keen, wide-awake mind is the fact that he discovered about one thousand new species of butterflies and other insects, and in this way earned much money for the use of the mission. His useful life came to an end in 1894, when he was only thirty-eight years old.

SAMUEL CROWTHER, the black bishop of the Niger, was born in the Yoruba country on the Gulf of Guinea,

CROWTHER

and when eleven years old was captured and sold as a slave. After many sufferings he found himself on a slave ship, which fortunately was taken by a British man-of-war sent out to capture slavers. He was educated in the missions of Liberia and Sierra Leone, and determined to devote his life to the uplifting of his own people in the Niger country. It was while he was engaged in this work that he was reunited, providentially, to his mother, brother, and sisters, who also had been sold into slavery. His mother became a Christian, and took the name of Hannah whose son was Samuel! In 1864 Mr. Crowther was consecrated first bishop of the Niger before an immense audience in Canterbury Cathedral. Until his death in 1891 at the age of eighty-two, his labors were unceasing both as an evangelist and organizer of missions, and as a translator, for he had extraordinary skill in languages. His work was done under the auspices of the Church Missionary Society.

ALEXANDER MACKAY (1849–1890) was the great Mechanic Missionary. The son of a Scotch minister, when he was only a three-year-old he could easily read the New Testament. The workmen on the manse would greet him: "Weel, laddie, gaen to gie's a sermon the day?" And always he would answer: "Please give me trowel. I can preach and build, same time!" When four years old he was sent after a small pick, but misunderstood and was later discovered struggling with an enormous six-foot lever, which he had brought fifty yards by dint of swinging it around end for end, two yards gained at every turn. His old nurse, on leaving, threw a leather strap into the mill-race, saying, "I'm nae gaen to let onybody whip my bairn when I'm awa'." The boy plunged in after it and was almost drowned. "How can I be good without a whip?" he explained. At seven, his reading lesson was the leading article in the newspaper; his reward for proficiency, to be told a missionary story; his choicest plaything a printing-press.

MACKAY

Mackay became an engineer, and got the best training in Edinburgh and Berlin. It was in Germany that he had what he described as "a new conversion," the call to be an engineer-missionary. Stanley's appeal for missionaries for the Dark Continent met his eye, and promptly in April, 1876, he sailed for Zanzibar as pioneer of the Church Missionary Society to Uganda.

Through all the fiery trials of the infant mission under that Felix king, Mtesa, and the cruel Mwanga, Mackay was the mainstay of the work. He opened up communication with the coast. While making the first road into the interior, he came one day to a deep stream too rapid to swim, flowing through an immense swamp. Sending an attendant after a rope by which he could lasso the opposite bank and pull himself over, he composedly sat down in the mire to master Haeckel's theory of molecules! At one time suffering terribly with fever, he was robbed of much of his stores, including the invaluable fever specific, quinine. This loss would have compelled his retreat had he not providentially met an Arab trader and obtained some quinine from him.

In Uganda, Mackay became, as he described himself, "Engineer, builder, printer, physician, surgeon, and general artificer to Mtesa, Kabaka of Uganda and over-lord of Unyoro." He built a wonderful house, introduced a cart, made a magic lantern, set up a printing-press, constructed a mighty coffin for the king's mother, was tailor, boat-maker, school-teacher, baker, sawyer, weaver, bridge-builder. "Man," wrote Mackay, "was made to be like his Maker, who made not one kind of thing, but all things." He taught the natives to work, telling them that God, when He made them with one stomach and two hands, implied that they should work twice as much as they ate. Winning attention by his mechanical marvels, he soon won hearts to Jesus Christ. Persecutions came. Converts were burned to death, chanting in the fire a Christian hymn, "Daily, daily sing the praises."

The missionary was driven out of the country to a very unhealthy region, where, always feeble, he did not long live. On February 8, 1890, this "modern Livingstone," as Stanley called him, passed from the scene of his manifold toils.

JAMES HANNINGTON was a lively English lad who won for himself the nickname of " Mad Jim," blowing the thumb off his left hand with powder designed for a wasps' nest, hanging when seven years old from the top of a mast, and finding it exceedingly difficult in later years to get through college. This gallant young fellow set out, in 1882, to reinforce the Uganda mission, which had lost so HANNINGTON many at the hands of fever and of murderous natives. Sickness drove him back to England, where he was consecrated Bishop of Equatorial Africa, and returned again in 1885. Unfortunately he approached Uganda from the north side of Lake Victoria Nyanza, and the natives counted every one their foe that came from that direction. Hannington was set upon and murdered after a week of horrible torture, and only four of his party of fifty escaped. He was only fifty-eight years old. His successor, *Bishop H. P. Parker*, died from fever in 1888, as soon as he reached his field. His successor is *Bishop Tucker*, a grand laborer, under whose care Uganda is now one of the most promising mission fields in all the world. *George L. Pilkington*, a student of Cambridge University, was among those that, in 1890, took up the work of Mackay, but his brilliant and consecrated life was cut short by mutinous natives in 1897.

THE UNITED PRESBYTERIAN CHURCH is the only American church with missions in Egypt. Upon Egypt and India all the missionary activity of that church is centred. The mission was begun at Cairo in 1854 by Messrs. McCague and Barnet, and has won a powerful influence throughout that ancient land among the Mohammedans as well as the Copts. There are four presbyteries, to which are attached as church-members and adherents more than twenty-five thousand natives. There is an American force of 58 with more than a hundred native assistants, together with 333 teachers at work in the mission schools. Perhaps the chief glory of the mission is the college at Asyut, which, with its more than 600 students, is the leading African institution of higher education for the natives. The Egyptian mission of the United Presbyterians has recently extended into the Soudan.

OTHER MISSIONS, all of great hopefulness, are the following : *The African M. E. Church* began their mission in Sierra Leone in 1886. *The Southern Presbyterian Church* founded their mission on the Upper Congo in 1891. It is a thousand miles by river from the coast. *The Southern Baptists*, after noble labors in Liberia, closed that mission and concentrated their efforts upon their mission to the Yoruba country at the mouth of the Niger — a mission opened in 1850 largely through the zealous toil of Rev. T. J. Bowen, and since maintained successfully, though with the sacrifice of many lives to the African fever. *The Protestant Episcopalians* support a mission in Liberia, which was opened in 1836. The first missionary bishop was Rev. John Payne. Referring to his service of a third of a century in that most unhealthful region, which left him "the mere wreck of a man," he wrote, " But I was no fool. I did follow the very footsteps of apostles, martyrs, and prophets." *The Lutherans* carry on the Muhlenberg Mission in Liberia, which was established in 1860. The nucleus consisted of forty children recaptured from slave-traders, named after well-known Americans, and educated by the missionaries. One of them afterwards became pastor of the mission church. *The United Brethren* have since 1855 maintained a mission on Sherbro Island, off the coast of Sierra Leone, West Africa. *The Canadian Congregationalists*, since 1885, have carried on a mission at Bailundu, in the Portuguese country, West Central Africa. *The Seventh Day Adventists* have work in South Africa and on the West Coast. *The Christian and Missionary Alliance* labors on the Congo and in the Soudan. *The Moravians*, who furnished the pioneer missionary to Africa, still labor in the south, and also in German East Africa. *The Friends* are beginning a mission in South Africa. Work in Africa is also carried on by the *Wesleyan Methodist Connection* (Sierra Leone), *Disciples of Christ* (Congo), *Free Methodists* (Portuguese East Africa, Natal, and the Transvaal), *Free Baptists* (Liberia), and *Seventh Day Baptists* (Gold Coast).

XXI.

MADAGASCAR

MADAGASCAR has a missionary history second in interest to no other. It is the third largest island of the world, and would stretch from New York to Chicago, being larger than France and almost as large as Texas. It contains three and a half million people, chiefly of Malay origin and language; for the island itself, in plants, animals, and geological formation, is sharply cut off from the African continent near by, and akin rather to the lands across the Indian Ocean. Missionary effort is centred at Antananarivo, the capital, and the great central plateau.

DAVID JONES and **THOMAS BEVAN,** two Welshmen, were the first missionaries to Madagascar. They had been moved to enter the work by a dream of the great dark island which their godly teacher, Dr. Phillips, related to his class. " Now who will go?" he had asked, and at once these two made answer, "I," "And I."

The London Missionary Society sent them, in 1818. Within four months the fever that is the scourge of Madagascar's coast-line had killed their wives, their children, and Mr. Bevan, leaving Jones alone. With this sad beginning, the gospel grew, fighting against the native witchcraft, fetichism, impurity, and a brutality that was even destitute of a word for conscience.

The missionaries toiled for eleven years before baptizing a convert. Gradually the infant church gained power, until Madagascar's " Bloody Mary," Ranavalona I., came to the throne. She was about to send the missionaries out of the country. "What can you do?" she sneered as they pleaded with her. "Can you make soap?" They knew nothing of soap-making, but within a week the resourceful missionaries brought to the queen a goodly bar of soap made with their own hands, and thus won a respite of five years.

But in 1835 the storm broke. The missionaries were driven from the island, hastening first to complete their translation of the Bible. A noble young woman, Rasalama, was the first martyr, a spear being thrust through her as she prayed. From sixty to eighty others were also slain.

In 1849 fourteen Christians were lowered, one by one, over the " Rock of Hurling," a precipice of 150 feet in Antananarivo. "Will you give up praying?" each was asked, and when he answered, "No," the rope was cut and the faithful witness was dashed to pieces far below. One was heard singing as he fell.

Others were burned to death, others stoned, or killed by boiling water, or by the horrible tangena poison. Four nobles had just endured a fiery martyrdom when rain quenched the flames, and the awe-struck multitude saw a beautiful rainbow springing from the spot.

For a quarter of a century the persecution continued, but in spite of it all, our Saviour won men's hearts so that on the return of the missionaries they found nearly four times as many Christians as they had left in the entire island. This return came on the death of the cruel queen in 1861 and the accession of her son, Radama II., who proclaimed entire religious liberty.

The missionaries were led by that hero, Rev. William Ellis, who had visited and comforted the natives during their quarter-century of sorrow. One thousand persons were present at his first service. A beautiful stone church was built on the " Rock of Hurling," and another where the four nobles were buried.

Madagascar's first Christian queen, Ranavalona II., came to the throne in 1868. At her coronation the Bible took the place of the old heathen symbols. She burned the royal idols throughout the island. She gave her private fortune to buy freedom for Madagascar's 150,000 slaves. She was one of the noblest of earth's sovereigns. Under her lead the Malagasy hastened by thousands into the church.

Her last days were darkened by a war with France, which was bent on enforcing an ancient claim to the island. After a heroic struggle of four years, the natives compelled the French army to withdraw. However, during the reign of her worthy successor, Ranavalona III., the French renewed the attack, and in 1895 obtained control of the country.

This means Catholic ascendency and great loss to the Protestant cause. The London Missionary Society has turned over a large part of its work to the Paris Evangelical Society, a Protestant organization. The English Society for the Propagation of the Gospel also has important missions in the island, together with the English Friends, the Norwegians, and the Lutherans of the United States.

A SUMMARY OF MISSIONARY STATISTICS.

By Permission, from Beach's "Atlas of Protestant Missions."

Countries.	FOREIGN MISSIONARIES, INCLUDING PHYSICIANS.					NATIVE WORKERS, BOTH SEXES.	STATIONS.		NATIVE CONSTITUENCY.			EDUCATIONAL.				MEDICAL.			
	Ordained, men.	Unordained, men.	Missionaries' wives.	Other missionary women.	Total foreign missionaries.	Native workers, both sexes.	Where missionaries reside.	Outstations, or substations.	Communicants.	Adherents, not communicants.	Total native constituency.	Day-schools.	Pupils in same.	Higher institutions.	Students in same.	Foreign male physicians.	Foreign women physicians.	Hospitals or dispensaries.	Patients during year reported.
The Aborigines of America	305	99	188	221	813	413	371	177	17651	14875	32526	201	5307	35	780	16	4	12	6768
Mexico	62	18	64	66	210	547	98	434	20769	17000	37769	148	7073	18	2217	8	.	4	200
Central America	40	11	38	13	102	293	48	57	4969	6454	11423	50	2617	.	163	1	.	1	.
The West Indies	200	34	159	51	444	473	236	578	68807	170773	239580	494	54608	8	943	2	1	.	.
South America	243	140	211	88	682	1687	223	352	37843	55173	93016	200	16437	14	1003	6	1	14	1212
Oceania	129	31	108	70	338	3058	196	1924	75681	277458	353139	2756	72638	38	.	14	2	13	.
New Zealand and Australian Aborigines and New Guinea	54	22	36	23	135	548	97	105	4958	28942	33900	101	4451	3	82	7	1	10	423
Malay Archipelago, or Malaysia	158	17	110	20	305	1553	135	524	37746	56494	94240	393	19190	15	250	6	1	8	6280
Japan and its Outlying Islands	252	40	232	248	772	1817	247	853	42835	41559	84394	148	8794	54	3735	14	7	13	16437
Korea	51	14	40	36	141	157	26	354	8288	2042	10330	43	601	.	113	13	.	12	19993
China	610	578	772	825	2785	6388	653	2476	112808	91864	204672	1819	35412	170	5150	162	79	259	691732
Siam, Laos, Straits Settlements, and Protected States	52	26	55	31	164	275	31	38	4557	2718	7275	66	2166	8	1493	12	3	10	18869
Burma	66	7	70	59	202	1797	38	548	43420	91111	134531	585	16578	41	4440	2	2	2	.
Ceylon	94	52	19	64	229	3338	99	360	12887	18184	31071	822	60882	19	1347	9	9	17	8358
India	1169	464	899	1304	3836	41673	1257	5367	376617	591310	967927	8285	342114	376	24255	89	111	313	1209738
Persia	26	9	22	28	85	281	13	80	3120	79	3199	114	3060	.	70	6	6	6	99713
Turkey, or the Ottoman Empire	128	108	123	278	637	1865	122	526	168367	51244	219611	767	36119	51	3251	35	3	63	184737
Africa	1158	634	779	480	3051	6547	1032	5866	274650	576530	851180	3497	201473	94	3574	66	9	126	252175
Madagascar and other African Islands	99	36	98	51	284	204	102	1461	68207	103165	171372	3031	168177	42	1306	7	5	17	25827
Fields Practically Unoccupied	11	7	8	2	28	24	7	3	.	.	.	.	.	.	.	.	.	5	9143
Missions to the Jews	132	382	13	9	536	.	210	.	.	.	.	1	612	1	5	.	.	.	.
Japanese and Chinese in Christian lands	14	11	96	61	182	124	75	44	2855	872	3727	58	5392	9	462	45	.	35	.
Papal Europe	77	68	15	73	233	930	184	236	10007	18502	28509	106	7910	9	9	1	.	.	6300
Bible Societies	36	46	56	4	142	1213	61	.	.	.	.	38	1594	.	.	.	.	7	.
Sailors' Societies	97	175	10	.	282	76	210	1	.	.	.	.	.	.	.	.	.	.	2238
GRAND TOTAL	5263	3029	4221	4105	16618	75281	5771	22364	1397042	2216349	3613391	23723	1073205	1005	54648	526	244	947	2545503

DIRECTIONS

FOR THE USE OF THIS BOOK IN A CLASS

No one person, however active in mind and persistent in studious habits, can study missions as well by himself as he could in a class. Contact with other minds is always a stimulus. There are new ways of looking at things. There are the doubts and perplexities of others to solve. There is the experience of others to draw from. There is the enlivening clash of question and answer. And while this is true of all subjects, it is especially true of a matter so vital and up-to-date as the study of missions.

In few particulars has the church made a more important advance during recent years than in the matter of the organization of mission study classes, both for old and young. It has come to be widely recognized that it is not enough to hold missionary meetings, good as those are. The information gained therefrom is too likely to be scrappy, and, in any event, rather the possession of the leader of the meeting and the few that prepare papers or addresses, than the common acquisition of all.

Every young people's society and every woman's missionary society (alas, that it should sound so strange to add, "and every *man's* missionary society!) should organize a mission study class. Make it as large as possible. If it can be made to include the entire society, all the better. But do not be discouraged though it must begin with a few. Insist that all the members shall be in earnest, whether it be large or small.

For the leader you will not need a person learned in missions so much as a good executive, able to set others to work, and keep them at it. Enough work is mapped out in the following pages to occupy the energies of the most ambitious class. What is needed is some leader of vigorous personality, who will get the work done. Any person that will make a good president of your society will be likely, if he or she has the missionary spirit, to make a good leader of the missionary class, even without any more knowledge than is possessed by the average member of the society.

As to times of meeting, they should be regular. The meetings should be close enough together to keep up the interest, and far enough apart to give time for preparation. Once a week is best. Once a fortnight is second-best. This book is arranged for nine such meetings. The society may pursue this course during one part of a year, and then, after a rest, take up a second course.

Organize the study class by devoting one meeting of the society to the consideration of the matter. Let some one who has looked into the subject present the importance of mission study classes and an outline of the work to be done. Have copies of this text-book at hand to show the society. Describe with some minuteness the way the class will be conducted. Enlarge upon the advantages of missionary study. Give examples of the noble lives to which you will be introduced. Read from the book some of the splendid instances of heroism. Show what a grasp of the world's history, of geography, and of political and social conditions everywhere may thus be gained. Throw open the meeting for informal questions. Call for expressions of opinion from this one and that. Of course the plan will have been talked over beforehand in the executive committee and with the pastor, and you will have at hand a body of ready advocates. When all the questions have been asked, and the subject has been fully presented, call for the names of those that will join the class, each agreeing

1. To attend as regularly as may be.

2. To obtain his own copy of the text-book (except that two or more from the same family may use one book).

3. To prepare each lesson with care.

4. To do as well as possible the special work the leader may assign him.

5. To try to interest others in the class, get them to join, and cultivate the spirit of missions.

Write this agreement upon a sheet of paper, and present it for the signatures of those that will join, having already by previous conversation persuaded a number of leaders among your members to sign the paper, and thus "start the ball rolling." After the meeting go to each member that did not sign, and try to remove his objections and obtain his membership.

Order the text-books at once, that you may get to work while the enthusiasm is fresh; do not wait to complete the enrolment by the canvass, but send a second order as soon as you obtain more members, or, still better, provide yourselves with extra copies of the book. Perhaps you can persuade some convenient bookseller to keep the book in stock.

A regular time for the meeting of the class is essential, that the members may plan for it properly. A regular meeting place is also essential. Do not take the society meeting place if it is so large that the class will not have the feeling of sufficient numbers. It is better to meet in a room that is a trifle crowded than in a room where you will feel lonesome. A private house is best, therefore, for a small class, provided the house is centrally situated; but the church is best for a large class.

At your first meeting organize by choosing a class secretary, whose duty it will be to see that the class is well advertised by public announcement in the society meetings and from the pulpit, in the church paper, if there is one, and in the town paper or city papers, on bulletin boards, and in every other way. The secretary will also notify the members of any necessary change in the time of meeting, and any special features to be introduced. He will act as the leader's medium of communication in the assignment of special work to the members of the class. He should see absentees promptly, urge *prompt and constant* attendance, and in every way seek to maintain the class at the highest standard of efficiency.

A class artist, to draw the maps and diagrams, will be another useful officer. Perhaps you will be able to find more than one person, that the work may be divided. It will be well to obtain some missionary map of the world, such as is sold by most denominational mission boards, together with the maps of your denominational mission fields which your boards will probably be able to furnish. In addition to these, however, and even if necessary without these, your own home-made maps are indispensable. I have purposely allowed the maps in this book to go with my own rough and hasty lettering, in order to set before the classes no copper-plate model, difficult to imitate. Large sheets of manila paper, soft pencils of various colors, colored crayons, ink, and the ability to letter clearly — these are all you need. The gummed stars and the like, whose use is suggested so many times in the following pages, may be home-made, or may be bought cheaply from any stationer. Whatever maps are made should be copied by the class in their note-books, and it will be well if a perfect frenzy of map-drawing seize them, so that they will make in large size all the maps shown in this book and many more. There is no better way to fix mission-ary information than by the wise use of a map.

A blackboard should be at hand during the meeting, ready for all kinds of diagrams and off-hand illustrations; but the paper maps I have described should always be made, for permanent use and for review.

A class librarian will be another useful officer, for you will need a reference library. I have named in the following pages many books, but to avoid confusion I have placed a star before the names of about fifty books that are most likely to be useful if you can own but a few. Half of these are double-starred, to signify especial usefulness. It is not absolutely necessary, of course, to have any book but the text-book, together with what books the class may al-ready own or have access to; but it will be a great advantage if the class can gather for the use of the society in later years and other studies, as well as for its own immediate use, as many as pos-sible of the books I have named. The reference lists are chosen from books recently published in America, and to be obtained through any bookseller, or they will be sent, postpaid, at the prices named, by the publishers of this volume. I have not named books published abroad, or books out of print. Neither have I been able to find space for the names of pamphlets, though many missionary pamphlets are full of meat. You will do well to write to your de-nominational mission boards, and ask them for a list of the pam-phlets and leaflets they have for sale; then provide yourselves with a complete set, together, of course, with the reports of the boards, reaching back as far as possible.

In preparation for the class meeting, every member should first read carefully the chapter assigned, and then test his knowledge by asking himself the questions on the lesson given in the following pages. This should be repeated till he is sure he has fixed in his mind all the leading facts. A definite time for study each day will greatly help. If the leader assigns extra work, the member should do it cheerfully and conscientiously. Keep a notebook in which, under the head of the different countries, you will jot down what is brought out in the meeting, and whatever additional facts you come across in your reading.

During this home study and during the meetings, indeed in the entire conduct of the class, the high spiritual purposes of the study should be kept in mind. Seek first the Kingdom of God. Our work, more than the study of geography, of fascinating biography, of world history, is the study of the progress of the Kingdom. Pray constantly, "Thy Kingdom come." Open your heart to the will of the Master. Ask ever, "Lord, what wilt Thou have me to do?" Pray for God's missionaries everywhere. Pray for the missionary spirit in your own life and in the life of your society and church. Pursue your study in this spirit, and put this spirit into your class work, and it will have results far more precious than any merely mental culture could bring.

The programme for the class meeting should be briskly varied, but the following may serve as a convenient outline:

1. Singing. Discover the missionary songs. Let the leader ask often, "What song is most suitable to be sung in connection with to-day's study of China, remembering the recent massacres there?" or, "We are to study to-day the life of Allen Gardiner; what appropriate song will you suggest?"

2. Bible-reading. Bring out during the class work the missionary passages of which the Bible is full. Seek out those that are less known. Ask such questions as this: "Of what Bible passage are you reminded by the life of Mackay?" Call often for verses from memory.

3. Prayer. Have much of this during the meeting, as well as at the opening. Often call for sentence prayers. Break off now and then in the middle of the lesson and have a season of prayer, asking God to impress upon you some great truth you have learned, or pray for God's blessing upon some especial field or worker.

4. Sketch of the country under review. Appoint for each meeting a different person who will be the "geographer" of the day. He will work with the artist in the preparation of the maps, and he will set before the class what the text-book says and what he can learn in addition concerning the size and population of the country, and its physical characteristics. Confine this exercise to ten minutes, and for many countries you need not take as long as that. Use the various diagrams and other graphic aids suggested in the following pages.

5. Questions by the class on the report of the "geographer." Additional information from any one.

6. Sketch of the social customs of the people, by a different member each week. He may be called the "sociologist" of the day. Try to give some idea of the character of the people. Do not merely choose the customs that are out of the way and curious, but those that throw light upon the missionary problem, the heart life of the nation you are studying. Five minutes, perhaps.

7. Questions and additional information as before.

8. Sketch of the religions of the nation under discussion. This also will be given by a different person each week, who may be called the "theologian" of the day. Do not attempt anything but a general outline — that is, do not go into discussions of the different gods of the heathen, and the like, but merely get a clear idea of the essential character and leading teachings of the chief religions of the world.

9. Questions and additional information.

10. Sketch of the secular history of the country, by the "historian" of the day. Make this very brief, as in the text-book, and confine it strictly to those points that bear upon missionary history.

11. Questions and further information.

12. Outline of missionary biographies, by the "biographer" of the day. If you can rely on the class for the faithful study of the matter given in the text-book, the biographer may take up some one of the many biographical sketches given in each chapter, and enlarge upon it from his fuller reading.

13. Questions and additional facts about any of the missionaries treated in the lesson.

14. General review of the course of missionary history in the country studied, together with especial attention to the missions of your own denomination there. This exercise should be conducted by the leader, who may obtain others from time to time to take his place if the town contains persons especially fitted to speak upon certain countries or fields. In this part of the subject make full use of the various graphical aids suggested in the book and in the following pages.

15. Questions and discussion.

16. Reading of special papers or giving of special talks upon any of the themes for further study suggested under each lesson. If you are able to take up only one of these at each meeting, yet it will be a decided gain, and will give to your class work a largeness of outlook that will be very inspiring.

17. A question review on the work of the day, conducted by the leader or by some member of the class appointed to be the "examiner" of the day. Use the questions given in this book as a basis, but enlarge them and improve upon them. Do not omit this feature. Include each week the chief questions of the week before, especially those that were not readily answered then. Do not ask "leading questions," but, on the other hand, do not ask questions that require long answers. Make the exercise as brisk as possible.

18. Current events and missionary information connected with the country under discussion.

19. Closing prayer.

It will not be possible to carry out this programme in an hour, and if you find that you have only an hour for the class, you must omit portions of it, retaining the parts that concern most closely the matter contained in the text-book. If, however, you make sure at the start that only those that are in earnest become members of the class, I can safely trust you to take all necessary time for a full and satisfactory meeting. In any event, make sure of the mastery of the most important facts contained in the text-book, and hold everything else subordinate to that aim.

☞ In order to indicate the value and use of missionary periodicals, I have included in the following pages many references to recent volumes of *The Missionary Review of the World*, using the contraction M. R., followed by the year and page number.

☞ The books' names are numbered *seriatim*, and a reference to "No. 21" for instance, is to Book 21 in this list.

☞ All books named in the following pages may be obtained from the publishers of this book, and will be sent, postpaid, at the prices given.

☞ The Conquest Missionary Library contains ten of the best missionary books, The Missionary Campaign Library No. 1 contains sixteen, and No. 2 contains twenty, all different. They are bound in cloth in uniform sets, admirably printed and illustrated, and are sent by the publishers of this book, postpaid, for $5 for the first, and $10 for each of the other libraries.

LESSON I.

Introduction and India (Chapters I. and II.)

SUGGESTIONS FOR CLASS WORK

1. Get some one to draw an outline map of India. Place beside it an outline map of your own State drawn to the same scale.

2. Draw two triangles, the sizes representing the populations of the United States and of India. *Note* that in similar triangles the areas are proportionate to the *squares* of corresponding sides.

3. Draw two triangles, the sizes representing the number of missionaries in India (3836, including wives) and the number of ministers in the United States (147,113, not including wives).

4. Give to each of six members of the class a piece of paper on which is printed the name of one of the great India languages, and let these be pinned to the map at the proper centres of those languages. Later remove these papers, and at the close review by pinning them on again.

5. Give each member one or more sets of adhesive stars marked with the initials of the various denominations at work in India. Let these be pasted on the map at the places where the various denominations have their most important work, and as each is put in place let the scholar tell something about the work of that denomination in India. Call this the "star drill."

6. Adopt a similar plan for the great missionaries, except that their names should be printed plainly upon strips of paper, through which long pins should be thrust, making a tiny banner. This will be stuck into the part of the map showing where the missionary lived for the most part, while at the same time some account of his life is given. Review by removing these banners, and replacing them one by one. Call this the "banner drill."

7. Take a long, smooth board, and mark it off into twenty sections, each for one decade of the two centuries from 1700 to 1900. Call this the "decade board." Number each section with the date at which the decade began. Prepare strips of paper on which are plainly printed the names of the great missionaries to India and the principal missionary events. Get the class to pin these to the board in the proper decades. Review till it can be done readily.

8. Let each member of the class draw from memory a map of India, putting in the language areas, the localities of the great missionaries, and the principal fields of work of your own denomination; also of other denominations so far as you can.

TEST QUESTIONS ON LESSON I.

1. What are some of the discouraging aspects of the missionary enterprise?
2. What are some of the encouraging features of modern missions?
3. What should spur the church to greater missionary zeal?
4. What are some of the chief advantages to be gained from the study of missions?
5. In what country did modern Protestant missions originate? With what man?
6. Compare India with the United States in size and population.
7. What are the principal religions of India? The leading languages?
8. What is the caste system, and what is its bearing on missions?
9. Give a sketch of English rule in India.
10. Who was the first Protestant missionary to India? What points in his career are typical of the entire course of missionary history in India?
11. Who was the first English missionary to India?
12. What does the "Haystack Monument" commemorate?
13. Who were the first American foreign missionaries?
14. Among missionaries to India, who was the greatest poet? The leading educator? The greatest translator? The most brilliant orator? The chief editor?
15. Who was the pioneer in medical work for women?
16. What were the Gossner missions, and what have they done for India?
17. Tell the story of the Lone Star Mission.
18. For what is the Tinnevelli Mission famous?
19. What has been the characteristic of recent Methodist missions in India?
20. Name the greatest English missionaries to India. Scotch. Danish.
21. Of the American missionaries, name the best known among the Congregationalists. The Presbyterians. The Methodists. The Baptists.

22. What was the origin of the Week of Prayer?
23. Who was Rachel Metcalf? Isabella Thoburn? William Butler? Henry Plütschau? Christian Swartz? Samuel J. Mills? Royal Wilder? John Thomas? Harriet Newell? Lyman Jewett? Who is Jacob Chamberlain?
24. What is the Lady Dufferin Association?
25. What is the work of Pandita Ramabai?
26. Characterize Swartz; Martyn; Carey; Heber; Duff; Clough.

GENERAL BOOKS OF REFERENCE

** 1. Geography and Atlas of Protestant Missions (Harlan P. Beach), 2 vols., $4. The best single work on missions.

* 2. The Encyclopædia of Missions (Bliss), 2 vols., $12. A massive work, valuable, though published in 1891.

** 3. The Missionary Review of the World. An interdenominational monthly. Funk and Wagnalls, New York. $2.50 a year.

4. Report of the Ecumenical Missionary Conference, New York, 1900, 2 vols. Up-to-date views of all fields. $1.50.

5. Concise History of Missions (Bliss), 75 cents. Philosophical and comprehensive.

* 6. A Hundred Years of Missions (Leonard), $1.50. Picturesque and popular.

7. A Manual of Modern Missions (Gracey), $1.25. A study by boards.

8. Missionary Annals of the Nineteenth Century (Leonard), $1.50. A study by decades.

* 9. History of Protestant Missions (Warneck), $2. Scholarly, large views.

10. Foreign Missions of the Protestant Churches (Baldwin), $1.

11. Nineteen Centuries of Missions (Scudder), $1.

** 12. Two Thousand Years of Missions before Carey (Barnes), $1.50. The leading work on this subject. Miss Hodgkin's Via Christi (50 cents) is an admirable book, in smaller compass.

13. Primer of Modern British Missions (Lovett), 40 cents.

14. History of Baptist Missions (Merriam), $1.25.

15. Southern Baptist Missions (Wright).

16. Presbyterian Foreign Missions (Speer), 50 cents.

17. Missionary Fields and Forces of the Disciples of Christ (Lhamon).
18. Handbook of Methodist Missions (John), $1.50; larger work by Reid and Gracey, 3 vols., $4.
19. Southern Methodist Missions (Wilson), 60 cents.
20. Moravian Missions (Thompson), $2.
21. Moravian Missions (Hamilton), $1.50.
22. Lutheran Missions (Lawry), $1.25.
23. Lights and Shadows of Mission Work in the Far East (Chester), 75 cents.   Southern Presbyterian missions.
24. Christian Missions and Social Progress (Dennis), 3 vols., $7.50; with Vol. 4, compilation of missionary statistics, $4.
25. Protection of Native Races against Intoxicants and Opium (Crafts and Leitch), 75 cents.
** 26. Qpportunities in the Path of the Great Physician (Penrose), $1.   A fine review of medical missions.
* 27. Great Missionaries of the Church (Creegan), $1.50.   Includes admirable sketches of Coan, Goodell, Schauffler, Griffith John, Bridgman, Thoburn, Logan, Butler, Thomson of Syria, and Hannington.
* 28. Eminent Missionary Women (Gracey), 85 cents.   Fiske, Agnew, Swain, Reed, Rankin, Egede, etc.
29. Women in the Mission Field (Buckland), 50 cents.
30. The Heroic in Missions (Buckland), 50 cents.
* 31. Heroes of the Mission Field (Walsh), $1.
* 32. Modern Heroes of the Mission Field (Walsh), $1.   Two volumes of interesting biographies, the first, of missionaries before Carey.
33. The Noble Army of Martyrs (Croil), 75 cents.
* 34. Miracles of Missions (Pierson), 4 vols., $1. each.   Graphic accounts of the most notable events of missionary history.

REFERENCE BOOKS ON INDIA

* 35. The Cross in the Land of the Trident (Beach), 50 cents. An admirable text-book.
** 36. India's Problem, Krishna or Christ (Jones), $1.50.
37. Indika (Hurst), $3.75.
38. India and Malaysia (Thoburn), $1.50.

** 39. Mosaics from India (Denning), $1.25.
 * 40. Village Work in India (Russell), $1.
    41. Within the Purdah (Armstrong-Hopkins), $1.25.
    42. The High-Caste Hindu Woman (Ramabai), 75 cents.
** 43. Wrongs of Indian Womanhood (Fuller), $1.25.
    44. Among India's Students (Wilder), 30 cents.
 * 45. Lux Christi (Mason), 50 cents. A study of India missions.
    46. Seven Years in Ceylon (Leitch), $1.25.
    47. In the Tiger Jungle (Chamberlain), $1.
    48. The Cobra's Den (Chamberlain), $1.
    49. The Story of Tinnevelli (Pierson, in No. 34, Fourth Series).
    50. The "Lone Star" Mission (Pierson, in No. 34, First Series).
    51. Conversion of India (Smith), $1.50.
    52. Men of Might in Indian Missions (Holcomb), $1.25. (Zie-
        genbalg, Swartz, Hall, Scudder, Wilson, Duff, etc.)
 * 53. Life of Ramabai (Dyer), $1.
    54. Mary Reed (missionary to the lepers, by Jackson), 75 cents.
    55. Life of Butler (by his daughter), $1.
    56. Life of Heber (Montefiore), 75 cents.
** 57. Life of Martyn (Smith), $3.
    58. Life of Swartz (Walsh, in No. 31).
    59. Life of Duff (Walsh in No. 32).
** 60. Life of Carey (Myers), 75 cents.
    61. Useful articles on India missions.   M.R. 1901, 522 ; 1903,
        22.

ESSAY SUBJECTS AND THEMES FOR FURTHER STUDY

1. Lessons for us from the famous sayings of great missionaries to India.
2. Great revivals in India, and how they came about.
3. The Indian mutiny: its cause, progress, and effect on missions. (See any large history of England; also No. 9.)
4. The pitiable condition of Hindu women. (See Books Nos. 43, 53, 42. M.R. 1903, 342.)
5. Every-day life among the common people of India. (See Nos. 35, 40.)
6. Medical missions in India. (Life of Clara Swain in No. 28; also No. 26.)

7. Characteristics of the religions of India. (No. 36. M.R. 1903, 321.)
8. The Somajes and their significance. (No. 36.)
9. What missions have accomplished in India. (No. 36. M.R. 1900, 263; 1901, 654; 1903, 247.)
10. How missionaries reach the people in India. (Nos. 39, 40.)
11. The mischief of the caste system of India. (Nos. 35, 37.)
12. The physical geography of India. (No. 1.)
13. India's saint. (Henry Martyn, No. 57.)
14. Lessons from the first English missionary. (Carey, No. 60.)
15. Some of the wonders of Hindu literature. (No. 37.)
16. A study of Heber's hymns. (No. 56.)
17. The missionary purpose of the Week of Prayer. (No. 16.)
18. Triumphs of faith in India missions. (Nos. 49, 50, 53, 54, etc.)
19. The horrors of India famines. (M.R. 1900, 369, 537; 1901, 245.)
20. The beautiful story of Ramabai. (Nos. 53, 42. M.R. 1901, 338.)

LESSON II.

Burma, Siam, Tibet, and Persia. (Chapters III.-VI.)

SUGGESTIONS FOR CLASS WORK

1. Have three outline maps drawn before the class: (a) Burma and Siam, showing also the French possessions and the Straits Settlements; (b) Tibet; (c) Persia. Place beside each a map of your State drawn to the same scale.

2. Draw four upright lines, their respective lengths corresponding to the populations of the four countries we study. Point out how nearly equal they are, and compare them with the population of the State of New York (7,268,012).

3. Take the number of ministers in your town and compare it by means of a diagram with the number of missionaries in Burma (202), Siam (164), Tibet (0) and Persia (85). For each country make a square representing a million persons, and containing as many dots as there are missionaries for that number. Place in another square as many dots as there would be missionaries if the million were as well supplied as your own town.

4. Dot in roughly on the map of Tibet the course pursued in the two missionary attempts to penetrate the country. Mark waiting crosses at the places on the borders where missionaries are seeking an entrance.

5. Make two triangles of sizes proportionate to the populations of the State of New York and of French Indo-China, where there are no Protestant missionaries.

6. Indicate on the map of Siam the Laos country. Show Arakan and Pegu on the map of Burma, and on the map of Persia the Nestorian country and the three centres of American missions.

7. Mark Siam and Persia blue for the Presbyterians, and Burma yellow for the Baptists.

8. Carry on a drill for the great missionaries, as described for India (the "banner drill"). Place the Judson banner successively in the various regions where he labored and was imprisoned.

9. Combine the three chronological tables, and carry on a time drill with the "decade board," as described in the preceding lesson. Add the two attempts to penetrate Tibet.

10. Review some of the India drills.

TEST QUESTIONS ON LESSON II.

1. What are the most characteristic Buddhist countries in the world?
2. How does Lamaism differ from Buddhism?
3. What are the chief religions of Persia?
4. Who are the Shans? Karens? Laotians? Kurds? Luurs? Babists? Sufis? Parsees?
5. What was the most dramatic event in Burman missions? In the missions to Siam? Tibet? Persia?
6. What were the six leading characteristics of the great missionary, Judson?
7. What denomination chiefly labors in Burma? Siam? Persia?
8. What attempts have been made to enter Tibet?
9. What missionary bodies are now at work on the borders of Tibet?
10. Compare Boardman and Martyn.
11. Compare the work among the Karens, the Laotians, and the Mountain Nestorians.
12. Compare the attitude of the governments toward missions in these four countries.

13. What are the relations of the Chinese to missions in Burma, Siam, and Tibet?
14. How was the early history of missionaries in Siam connected with that of China?
15. What denominations other than the ones now leading have been at work or are now at work in Burma, Siam, and Persia?
16. Describe the influence of medical missionaries in opening up these countries.
17. What peculiar missionary service was accomplished by Caswell? Price? Mattoon? McGilvary? Bassett?
18. Who was Mirza Ibrahim? Ka Thah-byu? Nai Chune? Moung Nau? Chow Fa Monghut?
19. Where are the leading mission colleges named in this lesson?
20. Describe the character and work of Fidelia Fiske.
21. Who are the Nestorians?
22. What saying of Judson's is often quoted? What saying in connection with Fidelia Fiske?
23. Who was "The Apostle to the Karens"? "The Apostle to the Lao"?
24. What are some of the practically unoccupied mission fields of Asia?

REFERENCE BOOKS ON BURMA, SIAM, TIBET, AND PERSIA

62. The Golden Chersonese (Bishop), $2. Burma.
63. Ten Years in Burma (Smith), $1.
64. Soo Thah (Bunker), $1.25. A story of the Karens.
65. The "Wild Men" of Burma (Pierson, in No. 34, First Series).
** 66. Life of Judson (Johnston), 30 cents; (Edward Judson), 90 cents, $1.25.
67. The Kingdom of the Yellow Robe (Young), $2. Siam.
68. Siam (Cort), $1.
69. The Land of the White Elephant (Pierson, in No. 34, First Series). Siam.
70. Among the Tibetans (Bishop), $1.
71. Land of the Llamas (Rockhill), $3.50.
72. A Journey to Lhasa and Central Tibet (Dao), $3.50.
* 73. Adventures in Tibet (Carey), $1.50. Miss Taylor's diary.

74. With the Tibetans in Tent and Temple (Rijnhart), $1.50.
75. Persia the Land of the Imans (Bassett), $1.50.
76. Persian Life and Customs (Wilson), $1.75.
77. Persian Women (Yonan), $1.
* 78. Eastern Presbyterian Mission (Bassett), $1.25.
* 79. Western Presbyterian Mission (Wilson), $1.25.
* 80. Woman and the Gospel in Persia (Lawrie), 30 cents. Faith Working by Love (D. T. Fiske), $1.75. Life of Fidelia Fiske.
81. Life of Perkins (H. M. Perkins), 30 cents.

ESSAY SUBJECTS AND THEMES FOR FURTHER STUDY

1. What Christians may learn from Judson's captivity. (See Book No. 66.)
2. The story of the three Mrs. Judsons. (No. 66.)
3. Characteristics of Buddhism. (See any good encyclopædia.)
4. The glorious triumph of the gospel among the Karens. (No. 14. M.R. 1903, 298.)
5. Physical characteristics of Farther India. (No. 1.)
6. Success among the Laotians. (Nos. 16, 1. M.R. 1901, 355, 358; 1902, 50, 349; 1903, 273, 358.)
7. The people and country of Tibet. (Nos. 73, 70, 71. M.R. 1900, 185, 211.)
8. Two missionary sorties. (Nos. 73, 74. M.R. 1903, 262.)
9. The queen of missionaries to Persia. (No. 80. Sketch in No. 28.)
10. The life of Persian women. (Nos. 77, 76.)
11. A study of Omar Khayyam.
12. A study of "The Light of Asia" compared with the reality of Buddhism to-day.
13. How Martyn died. (No. 57.)
14. Zoroaster and the Parsees. (See the encyclopædias.)
15. The martyrdom of Mirza Ibrahim. (Nos. 79, 16.)
16. Medical missions in Persia. (No. 79.)
17. The Bible in Persia. (No. 78.)
18. Persia's present and future. (M.R. 1902, 30, 119, 759; 1903, 363.)
19. Babism. (No. 1. M.R. 1902, 771, 775.)

LESSON III.

Syria, Turkey, and Arabia.   (Chapters VII.-IX.)

SUGGESTIONS FOR CLASS WORK

1. Draw an outline map of the Turkish Empire, including Arabia, Egypt, and Tripoli, as well as Syria and Turkey-in-Europe, with Bulgaria. Place in one corner a map of your own State drawn to the same scale.

2. Mark the four missions of the Congregationalists, the Methodist mission in Bulgaria, the Presbyterian mission in Syria, the Friends' mission at Jerusalem, the three stations of the Reformed Church in Arabia, and the United Presbyterian mission in Egypt. The latter is studied under Africa.

3. The Turkish Empire has 637 missionaries, the United States has 147,113 ministers. Take two ribbons and cut them to appropriate lengths to represent the comparative number of Christian workers per million of the respective populations.

4. Indicate on the map of Arabia the localities of the various productions for which it is famous. Mark off the three classical divisions of the country.

5. As before, make paper banners with pins for poles marked with the names of the famous missionaries, and place these at the spots where they labored. An unusual number of missionaries to this region have been great travellers. Move the pins to indicate the travels of Fisk, Parsons, Thomson, Goodell, Schauffler, Lull, Martyn, Falconer, French. Much of this is only hinted at in the text, and must be sought in fuller accounts.

6. *Upon* an outline map of the United States draw, to the same scale, an outline map of Arabia. Draw two circles of sizes representing their respective populations. There are ten American workers in Arabia. How many would there be if Arabia were as well provided with missionaries to the thousand of the population as your town with ministers and their wives? Illustrate with two dotted diagrams, as in the last lesson.

7. The Congregationalists are a remarkably active missionary church. They send nearly one-third of their missionary money to

their great field, Turkey, where they support one hundred and seventy-three missionaries (119 female, 54 male). In the United States there are 645,994 Congregationalists, with 5717 ministers. Show by triangles of two sizes what proportion the present number of missionaries per million of the population in Turkey bears to the number the Congregationalists would be obliged to send if they were to supply Turkey as liberally as their own churches.

8. Mark with gold stars on the map the great mission presses and the colleges.

9. Shade with black the portions of the map where massacres have occurred. Do not forget Bulgaria.

10. Draw in one corner of the map a square from which rays stream forth, and write within it the names of the missionaries (such as Lull, Martyn, Falconer) whose violent or untimely death has consecrated the Turkish Empire to Christ.

11. There are in the world to-day about one hundred and fifty million Protestants, and about one hundred and seventy-five million Mohammedans. Draw a circle, divide it in this proportion, and color one part black. Scarcely an impression has yet been made upon the Mohammedan world.

12. Drill in dates with the decade board, as before.

TEST QUESTIONS ON LESSON III.

1. What countries are ruled directly by the Sultan? What countries are under Turkish influence?

2. Whence came the Turks? What is their religion? What are some of the other races inhabiting Turkey?

3. What are the Greek Christians? the Gregorians? the Druses? the Maronites?

4. Who were the pioneer missionaries to Syria? to Turkey-in-Europe? to Arabia?

5. Where have the most recent massacres taken place? other massacres? What has been the result of the Armenian massacres?

6. Who was Asaad Shidiak? Sabat? Kamil? Who is Madame Tsilka?

7. Name some of the missionary explorers of the Turkish Empire.

8. Name some missionaries of the Turkish Empire (including Arabia) that have died after only a brief but glorious service.

9. What missionaries to Turkey have become famous for their translations?

10. Where in Turkey are the great Christian colleges situated? the great mission presses?
11. What are the two great divisions of Mohammedanism?
12. What was the Hatti-Humayoûn?
13. Characterize Schauffler; Hamlin; Riggs; Falconer; French.
14. What denomination leads in mission work in Turkey? in Syria? in Arabia?
15. What are the four Congregational missions to Turkey?
16. Where are the Methodist missions in Bulgaria?
17. Describe the Armenian massacres.
18. Describe Arabia.
19. What made the life of Raymund Lull remarkable?
20. Tell the story of Sabat.
21. Why is it especially important to evangelize Arabia?
22. Tell the story of Keith-Falconer.
23. Why have the missionaries to Turkey labored chiefly among the Armenians?
24. What are the lessons of the life of French?

REFERENCE BOOKS ON SYRIA, TURKEY, AND ARABIA

82. Impressions of Turkey (Ramsay), $1.75.
83. The Turk and His Lost Provinces (Curtis), $2.
* 84. Among the Turks (Hamlin), $1.50.
85. Constantinople (Dwight), $1.25.
86. Letters from Armenia (Harris), $1.25.
87. The Armenian Massacres (Greene), $1.50.
88. The Rule of the Turk (Greene), 75 cents.
89. Ten Years on the Euphrates (Wheeler), $1.
90. Missions in Eden (Wheeler), $1.
91. Shidiak, the Syrian Martyr (Pierson, in No. 34, First Series).
** 92. My Life and Times (Hamlin), $1.50.
93. Autobiography of Schauffler, $1.
94. Life of Goodell (Prime), $1. Under the title, "Forty Years in the Turkish Empire."
95. Life of Riggs. (M.R. 1901, 267.)
* 96. Arabia, the Cradle of Islam (Zwemer), $2.
97. Topsy-Turvey Land (Zwemer), 75 cents.
98. Islam and Christianity, $1.

99. Raymund Lull (Zwemer), 75 cents; also sketch in No. 31.
100. Kamil (Jessup), $1.

ESSAY SUBJECTS AND THEMES FOR FURTHER STUDY

1. A genuine Yankee missionary. (See Books Nos. 92, 84. M.R. 1900, 788, 872; 1901, 31.)
2. The Martyr of the Lebanon. (Nos. 91, 16.)
3. The most cosmopolitan city in the world. (No. 85.)
4. The story of Mohammed. (See any encyclopædia.)
5. The beliefs of Mohammedans. (Encyclopædias.)
6. Sufferings and heroism in the Armenian massacres (Nos. 86, 87, 88.)
7. The various religions and races in Turkey. (No. 1. M.R. 1901, 746, 839, 920.)
8. The mission press at Beirut. (No. 16.)
9. A study of the Talmud.
10. The most famous missionary captivity. (Report of the American Board for 1902. M.R. 1902, 451.)
11. One of the most romantic of missionary lives. (No. 99.)
12. The story of Sabat and Abdullah. (No. 57.)
13. The story of Kamil. (No. 100.)
14. Arabia and its people. (No. 96. M.R. 1901, 321.)
15. Two missionary martyrs. (Falconer and French in No. 96.)
16. Missions for Moslems. (M.R. 1900, 540; 1901, 291, 731; 1902, 732, 741, 891; 1903, 52.)
17. Moslem women. (M.R. 1901, 886, 933.)

LESSON IV.

China. (Chapter X.)

SUGGESTIONS FOR CLASS WORK

1. Draw an outline map of China. Measure off upon it the distance from New York to Chicago and from New York to San Francisco, and mark these in blue to give an idea of size. Write in blue above Peking, "New York"; above Shanghai, "Chicago"; and above

Canton, "Denver." They are about as far apart as those American cities.

2. Draw a circle, and within it one only a fifth as large, to represent the populations of the United States and China. The areas of circles are proportionate to the *squares* of their diameters.

3. Draw two squares of the same size, representing 144,000 persons. Place in the American square 288 dots, representing 288 ministers to 144,000 souls, and in the Chinese square one dot.

4. Draw Kiangsu province, containing Shanghai, and beside it the State of Pennsylvania, which is of about the same size.

5. Make a "century board" like the "decade board" described under India, and reproduce upon it the diagram showing the four mission periods in China. Use the decade board to reproduce the diagram showing the century of Protestant missions in China.

6. Affix to the map at the proper places gummed stars of different colors to represent the missionary centres of the larger denominations and of the smaller ones so far as possible. Use distinctive colors, as red for the Methodists, blue for the Presbyterians, yellow for the Baptists, green for the Congregationalists, etc.

7. "Banner drill" for the great missionaries, as before.

8. Darken the map to show where the massacres have occurred.

9. Mark the map red to indicate the scenes of the three wars (the Tai-Ping Rebellion being one of the three).

10. Take a long board and fasten hooks in it. Place it horizontally, and hang upon the hooks strips of pasteboard, each bearing in plain letters the name of the missionary who was the pioneer in one of the countries already studied — Carey, Morrison, Judson, Fisk, etc. Call this the "pioneer board," and use it, as the lessons proceed, as a review, arranging and re-arranging the cardboard strips in their right order. Mark the proper date on the board over each hook.

11. Make two squares, one containing 3500 dots and the other one dot, to show the proportion of Protestant Chinese to the Chinese that have not yet received the gospel.

TEST QUESTIONS ON LESSON IV.

1. Contrast with China the United States in size and population.
2. What are some of the difficulties of mission work in China?
3. What are the four periods of missions in China?

4. Who was the pioneer of Protestant missionaries in China? Who were the pioneers from the United States?

5. What wars have interrupted missionary work in China? What were the causes?

6. What have been the steps in the opening of China to the world?

7. What two great massacres in China? Describe the Boxer uprisings.

8. What are some of the famous sayings of great missionaries to China, or connected with their lives?

9. Who was Tsai-a-Ko? Leang-Afa? Howqua? Li Hung Chang?

10. Who are some of the great medical missionaries in China?

11. Name the greatest medical missionaries of the countries thus far studied.

12. Who was Frederick Ward? "Chinese" Gordon?

13. What were the five "Treaty Ports"?

14. What country sent the first Protestant missionary to China? to India? to Burma? etc.

15. Who were the leading literary workers among the missionaries to China?

16. Who was the great missionary to Formosa? to Mongolia?

17. Who were the great travellers among missionaries to China?

18. For what is William Murray famous? J. Hudson Taylor? F. D. Gamewell?

19. What connection had the Malay peninsula with early Chinese missions?

20. In what part of China are the most missionaries?

21. What missionary career in China do you think the most romantic? Why?

22. Who are the great Presbyterian missionaries to China? Congregational? Methodist? Baptist? etc.

23. What is the most important mission press in China?

REFERENCE BOOKS ON CHINA

** 101. Dawn on the Hills of T'Ang (Beach), 50 cents. A comprehensive text-book on missions in China.

** 102. China and the Chinese (Nevius), $1.50. An excellent general description.

** 103. Chinese Characteristics (Smith), $2.

104. Village Life in China (Smith), $2.

105. The Yangtze Valley and Beyond (Bishop), $6.

106. A Cycle of Cathay (Martin), $2.
107. The Lore of Cathay (Martin), $2.50.
108. Dragon, Image, and Demon (Du Bose), $1. Chinese religions.
109. History of Chinese Literature (Giles), $1.25.
110. The Chinese Boy and Girl (Headland), $1.
111. Among the Mongols (Gilmour), $1.25.
112. Mission Methods in Manchuria (Ross), $1.
* 113. From Far Formosa (Mackay), $1.25.
114. Modern Marvels in Formosa (Pierson, in No. 34. Second Series).
115. Murray's Work for the Blind (Pierson, in No. 34. First Series).
116. China in Convulsion (Smith), 2 vols., $5.
117. China and the Boxers (Beals), 60 cents.
118. The Tragedy of Paotingfu (Ketler), $2.
119. The Siege in Peking (Martin), $1.
120. Fire and Sword in Shansi (Edwards), $1.50.
121. Chinese Heroes (Headland), $1.
122. The Marvelous Providence of 'God in the Siege of Peking (Fenn), 5 cents.
123. Story of the China Inland Mission (Guinness), 2 vols. Published in England.
124. Life of Nevius (by his wife), $2.
** 125. Life of Gilmour (Lovett), $1.75; (Bryson), 50 cents.
126. Gilmour and His Boys (Lovett), $1.25.
** 127. Life of Morrison (Townsend), 75 cents.
128. Life of John (Robson), 75 cents.
129. Life of S. W. Williams. (M.R. 1901, 123.)
130. Peter Parker. (M.R. 1902, 569.)
131. Gilmour. (M.R. 1903. 81.)
132. Useful articles on China. (M.R. 1900, 99, 593, 864.)
133. China's Only Hope, 75 cents.
* 134. Life of Mackenzie (Bryson), $1.50.

ESSAY SUBJECTS AND THEMES FOR FURTHER STUDY

1. The difficult Chinese language. (See Book No. 102.)
2. Chinese characteristics. (No. 103.)
3. Famines in China, and how the missionaries relieve them. (No. 124.)

4. Religions of China. (Articles in the encyclopædias on Confucianism, Buddhism, and Taoism; also Books Nos. 1, 108. M.R. 1900, 711.)

5. Physical resources of China. (No. 1.)

6. Chinese literary examinations. (No. 102.)

7. The Tai-Ping Rebellion. (Nos. 101, 102.)

8. Catholic missions of China. (No. 102.)

9. The Boxer massacres, and the siege of Peking. (Nos. 116–122. M.R. 1900, 631, 657, 943; 1901, 8, 48, 81, 99, 103, 196, 206; 1903, 109.)

10. Study of the teachings of Confucius and Mencius. (Encyclopædias.)

11. The story of the China Inland Mission. (No. 123.)

12. Work for the Chinese blind. (No. 115.)

13. Splendid achievements in Formosa. (Nos. 113, 114.)

14. The beautiful character of James Gilmour. (Nos. 125, 126, 131.)

15. The career of Mackenzie. (No. 134.)

16. Views of a Chinese reformer. (No. 133. M.R. 1900, 36.)

17. The condition of women in China. (Nos. 102, 103, 104.)

18. Opium in China. (No. 25. M.R. 1900, 123.)

19. Gospel triumphs in Manchuria. (No. 112. M.R. 1900, 293, 746.)

LESSON V.

Korea and Japan. (Chapters XI. and XII.)

SUGGESTIONS FOR CLASS WORK

1. Draw a map showing Korea and Japan, together with the adjacent parts of China. Include in a red circle the regions in which the Chino-Japanese war was fought.

2. Place in one corner, as a guide to size, a sketch map of Minnesota, of the same size as Korea, or take your own State drawn to scale. Measure off on the area covered by Japan the distance from New York to Chicago. Mark in those two cities with blue.

3. Show by squares, one inside the other, the relative proportions of the populations of Korea, Japan, the United States, and China. Remember that the areas of squares are proportionate to the *squares* of their respective sides.

4. Draw from memory a sketch map of the region, showing China, Korea, and Japan, and indicating also the position of the Philippine Islands with reference to these countries.

5. Combine the two diagrams of the dates in the missionary history of Korea and Japan. Underscore with red the Catholic and with blue the Protestant portions of the diagram.

6. Use the "pioneer board" for a review of preceding countries in their beginnings, and add Allen and Williams.

7. Take circles of paper of different colors and paste them upon each of the three countries, China, Korea, and Japan, one color for each religion held by the people — as yellow for Confucianism, red for Buddhism, etc.

8. Place the drawing of a United States flag on the border both of Korea and of Japan, to show that our country was the first to make treaties opening these countries to the world.

9. Use the "banner drill" for the great missionaries.

TEST QUESTIONS ON LESSON V.

1. What is the leading religion of Korea? What are those of Japan?
2. Describe the Catholics' entrance into Korea, and their expulsion.
3. Do the same for Japan.
4. What were the relations between Korea and China? Between Korea and Japan? What great event changed those relations?
5. How did the opening of Japan to the world come about? the opening of Korea?
6. Characterize the Japanese people.
7. What denominations led the way in opening Korea to the gospel?
8. Who was the first missionary to Korea, and how did he effect an entrance and get influence?
9. What is the most important characteristic of mission work in Korea? in Japan?
10. What denominations are at work in Korea?
11. What denomination led the way in the missionary occupancy of Japan? Why?
12. Characterize the work of Hepburn; of Brown; of Verbeck,
13. Tell the story of Neesima.

14. Who was Kim? Rijutei? Min Yong Ik? Murata?
15. What is the Doshisha? the "Hall for Rearing Useful Men"?
16. What missionary physicians have been prominent in the history of Asiatic missions?
17. In what countries in Asia is Buddhism a leading religion?
18. Which Asiatic country is best provided with missionaries in proportion to its population?
19. What is probably the most interesting of mission fields? Why?
20. Who are the Ainus?
21. What have been the characteristics of recent missionary history in Japan?
22. What had missionaries to China to do with the beginning of the work in Japan? Why?
23. In what countries did Xavier preach? Where did he die? Under what circumstances?
24. What great missionaries reached Japan in the same year?
25. What cities are the missionary centres of Japan?
26. What descriptive names are given to Korea and Japan?

REFERENCE BOOKS ON KOREA AND JAPAN

* 135. Korea (Griffis), $1; (also the larger work by the same author, "Korea, the Hermit Nation," $2.50).
136. Korea and Her Neighbors (Bishop), $2.
** 137. Korean Sketches (Gale), $1.
138. Everyday Life in Korea (Gifford), $1.25.
139. Korea from Its Capital (Gilmore), $1.25.
140. "Self-supporting Churches in Korea" and "The Day Dawn in Korea" (Pierson, in No. 34. Fourth Series).
141. Tatong (Barnes), $1.25. A story of Korea.
142. The Mikado's Empire (Griffis), $4.
143. Religions of Japan (Griffis), $2.
** 144. The Gist of Japan (Peery), $1.25.
145. Japan, Its People and Missions (Page), 75 cents.
146. The Ainu of Japan (Batchelor), $1.50.
147. Japan (Newton), $1.
148. Life in Japan (Gardiner), $1.50.
149. Thirty Eventful Years in Japan (Gordon), 25 cents.
** 150. An American Missionary in Japan (Gordon), $1.25.
* 151. Japan and Its Regeneration (Cary), 50 cents.

152. Japan and Its Rescue (Hail), 75 cents.
153. Life of Verbeck (Griffis), $1.50.
* 154. Life of Neesima (Davis), $1.
155. Life of Xavier (Walsh, in No. 31).
156. Life of Brown (Griffis), $1.25.
157. Life of Perry (Griffis), $2.
158. Life of Harris (Griffis), $2.

ESSAY SUBJECTS AND THEMES FOR FURTHER STUDY

1. The Japanese language. (No. 150.)
2. Japanese religions. (No 143.)
3. The " hairy Ainus," and work among them. (No. 146.)
4. The story of the Catholics in Korea. (No. 135.)
5. The story of the Catholics in Japan. (No. 155.)
6. The American "war" with Korea. (No. 135.)
7. The war between China and Japan. (Newspapers and magazine files of the time.)
8. Japanese social life. (No. 144.)
9. Japanese art. (No. 142)
10. Japanese literature. (No. 142.)
11. Characteristics of the Japanese mind. (No. 150.)
12. Material progress of the Japanese. (No. 142.)
13. The people of Korea, their life and character. (No. 137. M.R. 1900, 261, 696; 1901, 688, 691; 1902, 180, 191)
14. Missionary life and work in Japan. (No. 150. M.R. 1900, 680, 688.)
15. Missionary results in Japan. (Nos. 151, 149. M.R. 1900, 283; 1901, 646.)
16. Self-support in missions. (Paper by Dr. Underwood in Book No. 4 and M.R. 1900, 443; 1901, 438, 440; 1903, 273, 358.)
17. How Korea was opened to the world. (No. 135.)
18. How Japan was opened to the world. (No. 157, 158.)
19. Missionary opportunities in Korea. (M.R. 1902, 664.)
20. The story of Neesima. (No. 154.)

LESSON VI.

The Islands. (Chapter XIII.)

SUGGESTIONS FOR CLASS WORK

1. Draw a map of the islands, including the East Indies and the neighboring portions of Asia. Surround each group with a light blue line, and draw a red line around the general divisions of the islands — Polynesia, Melanesia, Micronesia, and East Indies.

2. Indicate the different governments of the different groups by printing their names in different colors, the British islands in green, for instance, the French in red, etc. Where the ownership is mixed, as in the Samoan Islands, New Guinea, and Borneo, print the letters of the name part in one color and part in the others.

3. Fasten tiny American flags to the portions of the map where American missions are carried on. Place one also at Samoa, where the missions are English.

4. Place small streamers bearing the names of the great missionaries, as described in previous lessons, at the places where these missionaries labored. Move them from place to place as the missionaries journeyed. Use gilt paper for the banners of the martyrs.

5. Use the "pioneer board" for a review, adding the missionaries of the Duff, though really each group is so isolated that the beginners of the work in each deserve the name of pioneer.

6. Make a dissected map of the Island World, separating the principal groups. Pin these sections upon the blackboard, one by one, in the proper places, taking them in the order of entrance and occupation by the missionaries.

7. Draw in one corner of the map of the Island World a map of Georgia, whose area is equal to that of the three Pacific groups apart from the East Indies.

8. Show by two triangles the proportion between the total population of these three groups and that of New York City — 3,437,202. Remember always in such work that the triangles must be of similar form, and that their areas are proportionate, not to corresponding sides, but to the *squares* of those sides; *e.g.*, the areas of two right-angled triangles with hypothenuses respectively two and four inches would be to each other as four to sixteen; one would be four times as large as the other, and not twice.

TEST QUESTIONS ON LESSON VI.

1. What are the grand divisions of the Island World?
2. What is the area of the three Pacific groups? their population?
3. Characterize the religions of the islands.
4. Characterize their missionary history.
5. What group of islands was first evangelized? Under what circumstances? What is the present condition of missions there?
6. Give some account of the life and death of Williams.
7. Who was Obookiah? Thakombau? "Abraham"? Kapiolani? "Tamate"?
8. For what is the Duff famous? The Morning Star? The Endeavor? The Messenger of Peace? The Active? The Dayspring? (Paton's boat.)
9. What famous sayings are connected with missionaries to the islands?
10. Name the famous martyrs of the islands, and tell the circumstances of their deaths.
11. Why has the missionary history of the islands been so tragic?
12. In what portion of the islands have most of the martyrdoms taken place? Why?
13. What part have the native Christians taken in the evangelization of the islands?
14. In what group of islands, on the whole, has the gospel had the most powerful effect?
15. Compare the characters of Williams, Paton, and Chalmers.
16. What interesting events attended the introduction of the gospel to the Hawaiian Islands?
17. Tell the story of Captain Cook.
18. What mission to the islands has been closed, its work completed?
19. What three missionaries to the islands have had the most romantic lives?
20. What three instances of heroism in the history of the islands impress you most?
21. Illustrate from the history of the island missions the power of faith.
22. What nation owns most of the islands where effective missionary work has been done?
23. Describe the Congregational missions in Micronesia.

24. Describe the Methodist missions in the Fijis.
25. Describe the Presbyterian missions in the New Hebrides.
26. Who was "The Great-heart of New Guinea"? "The Apostle of the Maoris"? "The King of the Cannibals"?
27. What nation has done the chief work in the Malay Archipelago, and what is their chief missionary triumph?

REFERENCE BOOKS ON THE ISLANDS

159. Islands of the Pacific (Alexander), $2.
160. With South Sea Folk (Crosby) $1.
* 161. Transformation of Hawaii (Brain), $1.
162. Among the Cannibals of New Guinea (Macfarlane), 75 cents.
163. Among the Maoris (Page), 75 cents.
164. The Martyr Isle, Erromanga (Robertson), $1.50.
165. Lomai of Lenakel (Frank Paton), $1.50.
166. Life of Luther H. Gulick (Jewett), $1.25.
** 167. Life of Chalmers (Robson, 75 cents; Lovett, $1.50).
** 168. Life of Patteson (Page), 75 cents.
169. Patteson. (M.R. 1903, 337.)
** 170. Life of Paton (James Paton), $1. (I prefer this even to his autobiography, 3 vols., $2.50.)
* 171. Life of Calvert (Vernon), 75 cents.
172. Life of Marsden (Walsh in No. 32).
173. Life of Hunt (Walsh in No. 32).
** 174. Life of Williams (Ellis), 75 cents.

ESSAY SUBJECTS AND THEMES FOR FURTHER STUDY

1. The physical geography of the Island World. (Nos. 1, 159.)
2. The races in the Island World. (No. 1. M.R. 1901, 111.)
3. The religions of the Island World. (No. 1.)
4. A study of cannibalism. (No. 171.)
5. A study of providence in missions. (No. 161.)
6. How to deal with savage tribes. (Nos. 167, 162. M.R. 1901, 490, 598, 835; 1902, 481, 591, 669.)
7. The power of simple manliness, as shown in the life of Paton. (Nos. 170, 165.)

8. Missionary enthusiasm, as shown in the life of Patteson. (Nos. 168, 169.)
9. The iniquities of the foreign traders in the South Seas. (No. 170.)
10. Mission work in Malaysia. (No. 1. M.R. 1901, 821.)
11. The Australian aborigines. (No. 1. M.R. 1902, 495; 1903, 3.)
12. Erromanga — a typical island. (No. 164. M.R. 1900, 507.)
13. "The Africaner of the Fijis." (Nos. 171, 173.)
14. The unoccupied regions of the Pacific.
15. Missions among the Maoris. (No. 163. M.R. 1902, 326.)

LESSON VII.

Spanish America. (Chapters XIV.-XVII.)

SUGGESTIONS FOR CLASS WORK

1. Draw an outline map of all Spanish America, including Mexico, Central America, and the West Indies. Letter Brazil with a distinctive color, to indicate its Portuguese origin. Letter with different colors the British, Dutch, French, and Danish possessions on the continent and among the islands.

2. Draw in Central America the route of the interoceanic canal, and show its relation to missions.

3. Place in a corner of the map a map of Texas drawn to the same scale, or a map of the United States. Lay off upon Brazil the distance from New York to Chicago. Do the same for Chile.

4. Draw an outline map of Chile upon the same scale as a map of the United States, cut it out, and lay it upon the map of the United States.

5. Draw a circle representing the combined populations of the United States and of South America. Divide the circle into two parts proportioned to the two populations.

6. Show the neglected state of South America by taking two squares, each representing a million persons, and place in each as many dots as the respective countries possess Protestant ministers per million of the population. The population of the United States is seventy-seven millions. There are 682 missionaries in South America, including missionaries' wives.

7. Use the "pioneer board," taking Gardiner as the South American pioneer. The Moravians preceded him in the north, but Gardiner was the real pioneer of the South American missionary movement.

8. Place stars of different colors upon the map in the various countries where the different denominations are at work. Indicate by paper streamers, as before, the places where the great missionaries labored. Use a gilt banner for Gardiner.

9. Shade the map over the countries where least missionary work has been done, *i.e.*, from Bolivia north, including Venezuela.

10. Prepare slips of paper, each bearing the name of some division of South America, or Central America, the West Indies, or Mexico. Let the members of the class draw these slips, and each tell what he knows about the country he has drawn.

TEST QUESTIONS ON LESSON VII.

1. Describe the work of the Moravians in the West Indies.
2. Describe the work of the Moravians in South America.
3. Describe the work of the Moravians in Central America.
4. What are the secrets of the missionary power of the Moravian church?
5. What bodies of Christians are at work in the West Indies?
6. What work did Dr. Coke accomplish?
7. Why is South America called "The Neglected Continent"? Illustrate.
8. What especial claim on the United States has Spanish America?
9. What are the characteristics of Catholicism in Spanish America?
10. What is the condition of the South and Central American Indians?
11. What Oriental races are to be found in Spanish America? in what parts?
12. What is the dominant language in South America? What language comes next?
13. Why may we expect South America to become a thickly settled continent?
14. Tell the story of the Huguenots in Brazil.
15. Tell the splendid story of Allen Gardiner.
16. In what parts of South America are Presbyterian missions the strongest? Methodist missions? Baptist? Episcopalian?

17. Who was the Baptist pioneer in South America? the Presbyterian? the Methodist? the Episcopal?
18. What do you know about Mongiardino? Penzotti? Bryant? Aguilas? Gomez? Monreal?
19. What is especially to be remembered concerning Louis Dähne? Mary Hartmann? John Boles? Chamberlain? Bagby? Erwin? Matilda Rankin? Westrup?
20. What missionaries to Spanish America have had to endure much persecution?
21. Who was "the Cain of America"? the "Livingstone of South America"? "the Founder of the Republic"?
22. What is "Dead Man's Land"? "the Mosquito Coast"? "the Rich Coast"?
23. What denominations have missions in Central America?
24. Describe the population of Mexico. Who are the Mestizos?
25. Describe the climate and physical resources of Mexico.
26. Tell about the work of the Protestant pioneer in Mexico.
27. Give an account of the early persecutions in Mexico.

BOOKS OF REFERENCE ON SOUTH AMERICA, CENTRAL AMERICA, MEXICO, AND THE WEST INDIES

175. South America (Butterworth), $2.
176. Our South American Cousins (Taylor), $1.
* 177. Latin America (Brown), $1.20. A topical survey of the missions.
** 178. Protestant Missions in South America (Beach and others), 50 cents. A survey by fields.
179. South America, the Neglected Continent (Millard and Guinness), 75 cents.
180. The Bible in Brazil (Tucker), $1.25.
181. About Mexico, Past and Present (Johnson), $1.50.
* 182. Twenty Years Among the Mexicans (Rankin), $1.25.
183. Sketches of Mexico (Butler), $1.
184. Jamaica and the Friends' Mission (Bowles), 50 cents.
185. Izilda (Barnes), $1.25. A story of Brazil.
186. Ninito (Barnes), 90 cents. A story of Mexico.
187. Gardiner (Walsh in No. 32).
188. Useful articles on missions in Spanish America. (M.R. 1900, 859, 936; 1901, 168, 450, 808; 1902, 805, 856, 881; 1903, 132, 401.)

ESSAY SUBJECTS AND THEMES FOR FURTHER STUDY

1. A sketch of the political history of South America. (No. 175. M.R. 1902, 356.)
2. The condition of the South American Indian. (No. 177.)
3. Catholicism in Latin America. (No. 177.)
4. The present problem in Latin America. (No. 177. M.R. 1901, 856; 1902, 753.)
5. The physical geography of South America. (No. 1.)
6. Moravian missions in the West Indies. (Nos. 20, 21.)
7. Moravian missions in South America. (Nos. 20, 21.)
8. The heroic life of Allen Gardiner. (No. 187.)
9. Protestantism in Mexico. (Nos. 182, 183. M.R. 1900, 194; 1902, 195, 416.)
10. The Cross in the land of the Incas. (Nos. 1, 178.)
11. Mr. Grubb among the Indians. (No. 179.)
12. South America's missionary need. (No. 179.)

LESSON VIII.

Europe and Greenland. (Chapters XVIII. and XIX.)

SUGGESTIONS FOR CLASS WORK

1. Draw a map of Greenland, placing in one corner a map of your own State drawn to the same scale.
2. Show the localities where Egede and the Moravians worked.
3. Make a dissected map of Europe, and pin the various pieces to the blackboard in the proper places, taking them in the order in which mission work from America began in the several countries.
4. Place upon each country gummed circles of different colors representing the different American denominations at work there.
5. Use the "pioneer board" and the "decade board," as before.
6. Use the "banner drill" for the leading missionaries, as before.
7. Draw arrows on the various countries as you study the persecution of the missionaries there.
8. Pin upon the map small drawings or pictures of houses at the places where American Protestants have important schools or other missionary buildings.

TEST QUESTIONS ON LESSON VIII.

1. How early was Greenland converted to Christianity?
2. Tell the story of Hans Egede.
3. Tell the story of Moravian missions in Greenland.
4. What is the present religious condition of Greenland?
5. Give an account of Jonas King.
6. What other missionary work has been done for Greece?
7. What two denominations are at work in Bulgaria?
8. Tell about the Molokans.
9. What denominations are at work in Austria? Tell about persecutions there.
10. What denominations are at work in Italy? What was the beginning of Protestant work there? What is its present condition?
11. What are the McAll missions? What was their origin?
12. What other Protestant work is carried on in France by Americans?
13. What American Protestant work has been done in Spain? How was this work affected by our war with Spain?
14. What was the beginning of Baptist work in Germany? of Methodist work?
15. Tell about the persecution of Protestants in Germany.
16. What two American denominations have missions in Switzerland?
17. What was the origin of Methodist work for Scandinavia? Into what four countries has it spread?
18. Describe the Baptist missions in Scandinavia.
19. Describe the Baptist missions in Russia.
20. In what part of Europe have the Protestants been most severely persecuted?
21. Tell about Dr. Kalopothakes; Elieff; Julia Most; Adlof; Oncken; Müller; Nast; Hedstrom; Wiberg.
22. Where are these Protestant papers published: "The Star of the East"? "Il Testimonio"? "Der Evangelist"? "Kristelig Tidende"?
23. Where in Europe are famous mission schools carried on by the Episcopalians? Methodists? Congregationalists? Baptists?
24. Who were the Methodist pioneers in the various European countries? the Baptist? the Congregationalist?

REFERENCE BOOKS ON EUROPE AND GREENLAND

189. Spain and Her People (Zimmerman), $2.
190. Modern Spain (Hume), $1.50.
* 191. Italy and the Italians (Taylor), $1.50.
192. Romanism in Its Home (Eager), $1.   Italy.
193. Evangelical Missions in Spain (Fenn, in No. 34.   Fourth Series).
194. The McAll Mission in France (Pierson, in No. 34.   Second Series)
195. The Situation in France.   (M.R. 1900, 34; 1901, 507; 1902, 204, 282; 1903, 87.)
196. The Situation in Germany.   (M.R. 1900, 610; 1901, 593.)
197. The Greek Church of Russia.   (M.R. 1900, 760.)
198. Missions in Greece.   (M.R. 1901, 770.)
199. Missions in Bulgaria and Macedonia.   (M.R. 1902, 54; 1903, 329.)
200. The Situation in Austria.   (M.R. 1902, 564.)
201. Amid Greenland Snows (Page), 75 cents.
202. Egede (Walsh, in No. 31).

ESSAY SUBJECTS AND THEMES FOR FURTHER STUDY

1. The history and condition of the Greenlanders.   (No. 201.)
2. The faithful life of Hans Egede.   (Nos. 202, 201.)
3. The wonderful work of the Moravians in Greenland.   (Nos. 20, 21.   M.R. 1900, 109.)
4. Evangelical missions in Spain.   (No. 193.)
5. Methodist missions in Europe.   (No. 18.)
6. Baptist missions in Europe.   (Nos. 14, 15.)
7. Congregational missions in Europe.   (Reports of the American Board.)
8. The story of the McAll Mission in France.   (No. 194.)
9. The life of Count Zinzendorf.   (M.R. 1900, 329.)
10. The situation in Italy.   (No. 191.   M.R. 1900, 377; 1903, 297.)

LESSON IX.

Africa.   (Chapters XX. and XXI.)

SUGGESTIONS FOR CLASS WORK

1. Cut two squares of pasteboard, one white to represent the area of the United States, and one black, and three times as large, to represent the area of Africa.

2. Cut two triangles of pasteboard, one white to represent the population of the United States, and one black, and twice as large, to represent the population of Africa.

3. Cut from white paper a circle with the radius of an inch. It will represent five hundred persons — the average pastoral charge in the United States. Cut from black paper a circle with the radius of thirteen inches. It will represent the eighty-two thousand persons that make up the pastorate of the average missionary to Africa, counting wives as separate missionaries.

4. Lay off on the map of Africa the distance from New York to San Francisco. Draw a map of England to the same scale, and place it beside Madagascar.

5. Color the map so as to bring out the locations of the various foreign protectorates.

6. The "banner drill" for the great missionaries.

7. The "colored star" drill for the denominational mission centres.

8. The "pioneer board" drill. The "decade board" drill.

9. Place gilt stars where Mackay, Hannington, Parker, and Pilkington died.

10. Place a gilt cross upon the region where Livingstone, the greatest of all missionaries, labored and died.

11. Place a map of Madagascar, drawn to the same scale, upon a map of the United States.

TEST QUESTIONS ON LESSON IX.

1. Compare Africa with the United States in size; in population.

2. What are some of the difficulties of missionary work in Africa?

3. What portions of the continent are as yet practically untouched?

4. What effect has the slave-trade on Africa? the trade in strong drink?

5. What are the "Protectorates"? Among what nations is Africa thus divided up?

6. What nation began missionary work in Africa? Why they?

7. Describe the mission of Schmidt; of Vanderkemp.

8. What are some striking sayings of African missionaries?

9. Who was the greatest of the early missionaries to Africa? Where did he labor?

10. Who was Africaner? Dingaan? Mtesa? Susi? Rasalama? Ranavalona I., II., and III.? Radama II.?

11. What was Moffat's nationality? Name other great Scotch missionaries.

12. What was Schmidt's denomination? Name other great Moravian missionaries.

13. Who was "the Black Bishop of the Niger"? Tell his story.

14. Who was "the Flaming Torch"? What was the characteristic of his missions?

15. What missionary is noted for his mechanical genius? Name other missionaries in other lands that have used similar talents.

16. Who was the pioneer of Baptist missions? Tell his story.

17. What well-known missionaries to Africa died after only a brief service?

18. What country is chiefly cared for by the United Presbyterians?

19. What are the centres of Congregational work in Africa? of Presbyterian work? of Baptist work? of Methodist work? of Lutheran work? etc.

20. What fact renders Abyssinia unique in missionary history?

21. What missionaries have labored in Abyssinia?

22. Tell the story of Bishop Hannington.

23. What were Livingstone's contributions to the welfare of the world? Why is he counted the world's greatest missionary?

24. Describe the island of Madagascar.

25. What nation led in the missionary work there? With what success? With what interruption?

26. What is the present condition of missionary work in Madagascar?

REFERENCE BOOKS ON AFRICA AND MADAGASCAR

* 203. Redemption of Africa (Noble), 2 vols., $4.

* 204. The Price of Africa (Taylor), 50 cents.

205. Sketches from the Dark Continent (Hotchkiss), $1.
206. Abyssinia (Vivian), $4.
** 207. The Story of Uganda (Stock), $1.25.
208. American Mission in Egypt (Watson), $2.50.
209. Daybreak in Livingstonia (Jack), $1.25.
210. The Congo for Christ (Myers), 75 cents.
211. A Lone Woman in Africa (McAllister), $1.
212. Reality Versus Romance in South Central Africa (Johnston), $4.
213. Forty Years among the Zulus (Tyler), $1.25.
* 214. Among the Matabele (Carnegie), 60 cents.
* 215. Madagascar (Townsend), 75 cents; (Cousins), $1; (Fletcher — "The Sign of the Cross in Madagascar"), $1.
* 216. Life of Mackay (Splendid Lives Series), 50 cents; (by his sister), $1.
217. Life of Pilkington (Harford-Battersby), $1.50.
218. Life of Good (Parsons — "A Life for Africa"), $1.25.
* 219. Life of Crowther (Page), 75 cents.
** 220. Life of Livingstone (Blaikie), $1.50.
221. Life of Cox (Taylor, in No. 204).
* 222. Life of Moffat (Deane), 75 cents.
223. William Taylor. (M.R. 1902, 609.)
224. Useful articles on Africa. (M.R. 1900, 417, 817, 920; 1901, 410; 1902, 403, 407.)

ESSAY SUBJECTS AND THEMES FOR FUTURE STUDY

1. The physical geography of Africa, and its bearing on the missionary problem. (No. 1.)
2. The races of Africa, their character and religions. (No. 1.)
3. Important events in the political history of Africa. (Files of *The Review of Reviews* and similar magazines.)
4. The African fever and its ravages. (No. 204.)
5. The African slave-trade and its horrors. (No. 219. M.R. 1902, 456.)
6. The evils of the rum trade with Africa. (No. 25.)
7. Four distinctive fields: Natal, the Congo, Uganda, and Egypt. (Reports of the Congregational, Baptist, and United Presbyterian Boards, and Books Nos. 207, 208, 210, 213. M.R. 1900, 18, 518, 604; 1902, 373.)

8. Lessons from African martyrs. (No. 204.)
9. Proof of what missions can do for the African. (No. 219.)
10. The story of Khama. (No. 214. M.R. 1901, 93.)
11. Missions in Madagascar, their trials and triumphs. (No. 215. M.R. 1900, 904; 1902, 436.)
12. A model missionary. (No. 216.)
13. The world's greatest missionary. (No. 220. M.R. 1900, 766.)
14. Stanley's explorations and the influence of Livingstone upon him.

If possible, take a day for the following: —

15. The twelve great missionaries. A review.
16. The most characteristic phases of missionary history in the various mission lands. A review.
17. Landmarks of missionary history (the missionary events that stand out above all others in each land). A review. (M.R. 1900, 241.)
18. Missionary martyrdoms. A review.
19. The great providences of missions. A review.
20. Missionary opportunities and needs of the present time. A review.
21. A conspectus of the missionary work of our own denomination. A review.
22. The Great Commission, and how it is being fulfilled, or, Christ in the missionary enterprise. A review. (M.R. 1900, 1, 43.)

Index

Indian mutiny, 14, 27.
Indians, 122, 123, 124, 125, 126, 129, 132, 136, 138.
Indo-China (French), 44.
Inglis, 106.
Italy, 153.

J

Jacoby, 157.
Jamaica, 143, 144, 145.
Japan, 88.
Jarrett, 133.
Jewett, 25.
John, Griffith, 77.
Jones, 181.
Judson, 18, 33.

K

Kalopothakes, 150.
Kamil, 64.
Kanarese, 14.
Kapiolani, 110.
Karens, 33, 36, 37.
Ka Thah-byu, 36.
Kayarnak, 148.
Kerr, 80.
Ketteler, 69.
Kim, 84.
Kimball, Grace, 59.
King, 149.
Knapp, 156.
Kols, 29.
Korea, 83.
Krapf, 172.
Kurds, 45, 47, 48, 58, 59.

L

Lamaism, 42.
Laos, 38, 40, 44.
Larsson, 158.
Lawes, 116.
Leang-Afa, 71.
Legge, 39.
Leyburn, 150.
Liberia, 171, 172, 175, 179, 180.
Liggins, 91.
Li Hung Chang, 80.
Livingstone, 169.
Logan, 114.

Lone Star Mission, 25.
Long, 151.
Loochoo Islands, 92.
Lowrie, John C., 24.
Lowrie, Walter, 74.
Lull, 61.
Lutheran (General Council) missions, 12, 29.
Lutheran (General Synod) missions, 12, 29, 165, 180.
Luurs, 45.
Lyman, 118.

M

Macedonia, 56.
Macfarlane, 116.
Mackay, Alexander, 63, 176.
Mackay, G. L., 79.
Mackenzie, 79.
Madagascar, 181.
Maibant, 84.
Malaysia, 118.
Manchuria, 85.
Maoris, 103, 104.
Marathi, 13.
Maronites, 51.
Marquesan Islands, 113.
Marsden, 102.
Marshall Islands, 114, 115.
Martyn, 20, 45, 62, 127.
Massacres, 50, 52, 56, 58, 67, 77, 85.
Matabeleland, 169.
Mattoon, 40.
McAll, 154.
McCague, 179.
McGilvary, 40.
Medhurst, 39, 71, 72, 119.
Medical missionaries, Number of, 9.
Medical missions, 24, 27, 30, 74, 79, 80, 85, 86, 167, 169.
Melanesia, 97.
Mennonite missions, 12, 28.
Merriam, William W., 56.
Messenger of Peace, The, 100.
Metcalf, Rachel, 29.
Methodist (North) missions, 12, 26, 27, 28, 37, 40, 56, 75, 81,